Reexamining Family Stress

RECENT VOLUMES IN . . .
SAGE LIBRARY OF SOCIAL RESEARCH

Reexamining Family Stress

New Theory and Research

Wesley R. Burr
Shirley R. Klein

with

Robert G. Burr

Cynthia Doxey

Brent Harker

Thomas B. Holman

Paul H. Martin

Russell L. McClure

Shawna Weiler Parrish

Daniel A. Stuart

Alan C. Taylor

Mark S. White

Sage Library of Social Research 193

SAGE Publications
International Educational and Professional Publisher
Thousand Oaks   London   New Delhi

For information address:

SAGE Publications, Inc.
2455 Teller Road
Thousand Oaks, California 91320

SAGE Publications Ltd.
6 Bonhill Street
London EC2A 4PU
United Kingdom

SAGE Publications India Pvt. Ltd.
M-32 Market
Greater Kailash I
New Delhi 110 048 India

Printed in the United States of America

Library of Congress Cataloging-in-Publication Data

Burr, Wesley R., 1936-
    Reexamining family stress: new theory and research/Wesley R.
  Burr, Shirley R. Klein: with Robert G. Burr . . . [et al.]
      p. cm.
    Includes bibliographical references and index.
    ISBN 0-8039-4929-4.—ISBN 0-8039-4930-8 (pbk.)
    1. Family—Pyschological aspects. 2. Stress (Psychology)
  3. System theory. I. Klein, Shirley R. II. Title.
  HQ518.B875 1994   93-21399
  306.85'01'9—dc20

95 96 97 10 9 8 7 6 5 4 3 2

Sage Production Editor: Megan M. McCue

Contents

Preface

This project began when Robert Burr (1989) decided to write a theoretical essay about family stress theories. He focused on the limitations of the ABC-X models of family stress and the advantages of using a systemic approach that was internally consistent rather than piggy-backed on top of the earlier positivistic model. He worked with Tom Holman and Wes Burr, and they became increasingly intrigued with the refined theoretical approach. During the 1991-92 academic year, the resources were acquired to add an empirical study to the theoretical essay Burr had written. The larger research team was then assembled.

We worked as a team in the design and data-gathering stages of the project, and divided into smaller groups that consulted with one another during the data analysis and write-up stages. The findings chapters were initially written by separate groups, thus both the responsibility and credit for good things and blame for limitations should go to Wesley Burr (Chapter 1); Robert Burr and Wesley Burr (Chapter 2); Robert Burr, Wesley Burr, and Thomas Holman (Chapter 3); Shirley Klein (Chapter 4); Brent Harker (Chapter 5); Russell McClure and Alan Taylor (Chapter 6); Paul Martin and Wesley Burr (Chapter 7); Dan Stuart and Paul Martin (Chapter 8); Cynthia Doxey (Chapter 9); and Shirley Klein and Wesley Burr (Chapter 10).

After the chapters were completed, Wesley Burr and Shirley Klein integrated many of the ideas, eliminated overlaps, and edited the numerous voices to read as one.

We express our appreciation to the many individuals who have assisted us in this project. We are especially grateful to the thoughtful and helpful critiques by Jay Schvaneveldt, Richard Gelles, Hamilton McCubbin, and Charles Figley.

Wesley R. Burr
Shirley R. Klein

ONE

Introduction

The main goal in this book is to take advantage of several recent developments and add new insights to the literature about family stress. The developments we think are useful include: (a) the introduction of several systemic concepts into the family stress literature, (b) the increasing sophistication in the methodology of qualitative research, and (c) the insights that have emerged from the debates about the limits and disadvantages of positivism and the advantages of several nonpositivistic methods of inquiry. These developments allow us to make several refinements in existing theories, add to them, and empirically test some of their newer ideas.

Another goal in this project is to accomplish what Olson (1976) has called a "triple threat." This means that we want to make contributions to theory, research, and practice. Ultimately, the practical contributions will be the most valuable because theory and research are merely the means of developing new ideas to enhance family life. We have tried to ask questions, gather data, and present findings that are comprehensible and useful to a wide range of practitioners, students, and, ultimately, families. We have included personal stories about family stress from individuals in the midst of the drama. These stories richly describe real-life experiences and illustrate family connections to the concepts of stress we are studying.

The chapters that report findings introduce several ideas of practical value. For example, Chapter 5 demonstrates more variety in the ways families respond to stress than has been found in previous research. If it becomes generally known, then this finding may help families maintain higher morale during stressful periods. Chapter 6 shows that some aspects of family systems tend to be more disrupted than others during periods of stress—and that some features of family systems actually tend to improve. Chapter 7 provides new information about which coping strategies families find the most helpful or the most harmful in different stressful situations. This type of information can assist families and practitioners who want to know more about how family systems react to stress, where to focus resources and attention to be the most effective, and where families encountering stress might find a "silver lining."

We have sought to make theoretical contributions in several ways. First, we have tried to clarify theories about family stress to achieve more internal consistency within the theories. We believe that many of the innovations of the 1970s and '80s were important contributions, although some are blurred because of conflicting theoretical foundations. When families think, adapt, change, choose, and decide as they cope with stress, they are using indeterministic systemic processes, and yet scholars have used older theoretical deterministic models to study these family behaviors. Our attempt to correct the internal inconsistencies that result from the conflict of combining two models accomplishes two goals. Second, in Chapter 2 we show further clarifications in both the deterministic and indeterministic theories, and we add several new ideas to the systemic theory.

Third, we have sought to contribute to empirical research by bringing quantitative and qualitative data to bear on several new theoretical ideas. More specifically, the data are analyzed to determine how universal the Koos roller-coaster pattern is as well as to identify alternative response patterns if the pattern is not universal. We also have data about how nine different aspects of family systems are influenced by stress. No previous research has tried to determine how different aspects of family systems may respond differently to stressful situations. We have used multiple types of stressors to determine whether some of the coping strategies that have previously been theorized to be universally helpful are always helpful. We have provided data about whether some coping strategies actually tend to produce harmful effects in family systems. Finally, we have provided data about whether families have a predictable pattern in the way they use coping strategies that are designed to bring about first-order and second-order change and a more abstract kind of change that is conceptualized as third-order or Level III change in family systems.

OVERVIEW

Here we describe the organization and key points of each chapter. Chapter 2 summarizes the paradigmatic orientation or basic assumptions that guided this project and suggests the use of Hegelian dialectic to understand the current debates about scientific paradigms. We then describe a synthesized paradigm that guided our thinking.

Chapter 3 describes the theoretical ideas that guided this project. It begins by discussing the differences between the ABC-X model and a systems-oriented model. We demonstrate that the assumptions in the ABC-X model are fundamentally positivistic, which makes them incompatible with the assumptions made in the indeterministic branches of family systems theories. After clarifying these differences, several conceptual and theoretical ideas are introduced, including some related to the systems model. For example, previous theories of family stress have not dealt with different levels of abstraction in the system processes. The model presented in Chapter 2 introduces the concept of levels of abstraction and suggests how this idea can help us understand how family systems respond to stress.

Chapter 4 describes the methods used in the empirical part of the project. In-depth interviews and observations were made with families who had experienced one of six different types of family stress. The stressors included (a) bankruptcy, (b) a child who was handicapped enough to be institutionalized, (c) a teenage child who was difficult enough to manage that professional psychiatric help was sought, (d) a child with muscular dystrophy, (e) infertility, and (f) displaced homemaker status.

The interviews were partially structured and audiotaped so that comments could be reexamined later. The interview responses were examined with a variety of techniques. Some information was coded and quantified for analysis with inferential statistics, but the majority of the time and energy in the data analysis was devoted to in-depth understanding of the patterns in the responses and variations in these patterns that would help provide information about the specific questions and issues addressed in the project. Thus the project was an attempt to integrate quantitative and qualitative research methods in a complementary manner.

Chapter 5 addresses two issues. First, is the roller-coaster pattern developed by Koos (1946) a universal pattern in family systems? It has been treated in the family literature as if it were the universally appropriate model for describing how family systems respond to stress. The investigators theorized that it is an accurate and helpful model for describing the way some families respond to stress in some situations, but that it is not a universally experienced pattern. The analysis of the data found that the Koos model operates 50% to 60% of the time and that four other patterns also were apparent. Second, how do families allocate their time, effort, and energy once they have encountered stress? Intuitively, we reasoned before the data were analyzed that families would allocate their resources in proportion to how seriously their functioning was disrupted. A majority of the families exhibited this pattern, but two other unanticipated patterns appeared in the data; this chapter will describe them.

Chapter 6 focuses on the question of how several specific parts of family systems respond to stress. We gathered data about how nine specific aspects of family life tend to change under stress:

1. marital satisfaction,
2. family rituals and celebrations,
3. quality of communication,
4. family cohesion,
5. functional quality of the executive subsystem,
6. quality of the emotional atmosphere,
7. management of daily routines and chores,

8. contention, and
9. normal family development versus changed or arrested development.

All of these specific parts of family systems may respond in the same way to stress. Or different aspects of the family might change in dissimilar ways. This question has not been addressed in previous research. Therefore, we do not now have any information about how specific aspects of family systems change as families cope with stress.

Several important findings are reported in this chapter. For example, our data suggest that stress tends to disrupt the emotional atmosphere and the quality of task performance in a large percentage of families, but the quality of family cohesion, communication, and marital satisfaction tend to improve simultaneously in a large percentage of families. There are, of course, many differences in the response patterns, but these model tendencies have not been identified in previous research, and they have important practical implications for helping families know what to anticipate and where to concentrate their attention and resources when stress occurs. This chapter also discusses the differential effects of the six different stress-producing events. The number of families in each situation is small, so these findings are suggestive at most, although variation itself is significant.

Chapter 7 examines the various ways in which previous scholars have grouped and classified the strategies that families use to manage stress. These have been called *coping strategies* in the previous literature; we also refer to them in this chapter as *management strategies*.

Our examination of the previous literature revealed considerable inconsistency and confusion in the conceptualization of these strategies. Large numbers of "lists" of management strategies have been compiled, and these include hundreds of strategies. Some lists are small, others large, and they only partially overlap. When we discovered this confusion in the way these strategies have been conceptualized, we decided that one useful task would be to try to create a more simplified and integrated conceptual framework of management strategies.

This chapter introduces a conceptual framework that we think
will help theorists, researchers, and practitioners think more effectively about the strategies families use to try to manage stress. We
identify seven different categories of strategies and show how several of these have meaningful subcategories. We then show how
these categories include the large number of fairly specific strategies that have been discussed in the literature. The result is a multi-
level conceptual framework that we hope will help clarify this part
of the family stress literature.

Chapter 8 uses the conceptual framework that was developed in
Chapter 7 to provide several new insights into families' stress management. Previous literature has suggested several coping strategies that are universally beneficial and several strategies that tend
to be disabling. Unfortunately, little data are available to justify
some of these conclusions. We therefore gathered data on the extent to which families used the strategies and what they felt the
effects of the strategies to be. The findings provide several useful
insights about which strategies tend to be highly used, highly helpful,
or disabling.

Chapter 9 begins to test one theoretical innovation suggested in
Chapter 2. Family systems theory has developed a conceptual
framework for differentiating between three different levels of abstraction in system processes. These conceptual innovations began
with the distinction between first-order and second-order change
introduced by Watzlawick, Weakland, and Fisch (1974). David Reiss's
The Family's Construction of Reality (1981) developed the concept of
family paradigms. These abstract ideological aspects of family systems involve more abstract systemic process than second-order
change. Several scholars have proposed a threefold typology that
has been recently described as Level I (first-order change and
transformation), Level II (second-order change, metarules), and
Level III (family paradigms, values) processes.

Robert Burr (1989) theorized that families encountering stress-
producing events first tend to use a wide range of coping strategies
that are designed to produce first-order (Level I) change. When
these strategies adequately manage the impact of the stress-
producing event, the family system moves ahead with other aspects of life. However, when the Level I strategies are not adequate,

families then tend to do one of two things: (a) try coping strategies that involve Level II or Level III change or (b) experience severely disabling stress. Thus we proposed that families show a developmental pattern in the way they manage stress. Data were gathered in the current project by means of a modified Q-sort that will provide insights about the developmental patterns in the way that families cope with stress. Findings in this chapter show whether these patterns are different with different kinds of stress-producing events.

Chapter 10 summarizes the practical implications of the findings in the earlier chapters. We also try to think more generally about where we are in understanding family stress and where we might want to go next. We also try to identify some of the questions and issues that ought to be addressed in future research.

TWO

Paradigms and Assumptions

Doing research in the social sciences in the 1990s is more complicated than it was a few decades ago. In the simpler era, we only worried about methodological concerns such as clear hypotheses related to a theoretical idea, defensible design, sampling, measurement, and appropriate statistical analysis. In recent years, however, many more scholars have raised concerns about more fundamental issues that deal with philosophical assumptions, metatheoretical perspectives, and previously unrecognized biases such as insensitivity to gender differences.

Now we also need to be concerned about such fundamental issues as the assumptions we make about reality, whether objectivity or certainty are possible or desirable, and whether we are searching for law-like statements about cause and effect. We also now realize the importance of clarity in stating the ultimate goals or objectives of our research. For example, are our objectives emancipation, critical theory, prediction, control, explanatory theory, or theory that is useful to practitioners? (See Jurich & Burr, 1989; Sprey, 1990, p. 24.) We also need to be consistent in the paradigmatic orientation we use (Capra, 1982; Doherty, 1986; Kuhn, 1970).

This chapter is our attempt to deal with these issues by trying to explain our views about some of these issues. This chapter is included for several reasons. First, our paradigmatic orientation influenced what we did in the later chapters, and many readers will appreciate the presuppositions being made explicit. Second, trying to explain our fundamental assumptions helped us in our struggle to understand and clarify our own presuppositions and goals. Third, the 1990s is a unique period in the evolution of family science in particular and the social sciences in general. Social scientists have tried to develop methods of inquiry that are useful in accomplishing our intellectual and practical goals, but thus far we have not been able to find a widely acceptable approach or group of approaches to knowledge construction. The positivistic approach was widely acceptable in the earlier decades of this century, but its limitations are becoming increasingly evident, and a growing number of scholars are searching for alternative modes of inquiry (Hultgren, 1989; Sprey, 1990). We are among those who search for more effective paradigms, and we hope our attempt to describe our "working solution" will contribute to the larger dialogue about these metatheoretical issues.

Before we begin our discussion of these issues, we make several preliminary comments. Our ideas about how to do science are still evolving and are being influenced by the ongoing dialogue about these issues. This makes our discussion here a "progress report" on where we are in our evolution and growth rather than a finished product. Because this is our first attempt to clarify many of our assumptions and goals, some of our ideas are not explained in as much detail or as clearly as we or some of our readers would like. Also it is likely that with further reflection and dialogue we will realize that some of our current ideas should be modified. Thus our discussion is a beginning attempt to explain a point of view that we think is shared by many other family scientists but not well articulated in the metatheoretical literature.

We acknowledge our dependence on the dialogue about these metatheoretical and philosophical issues. The dialogue has made us more sensitive to the existence of many modes of inquiry and has sensitized us to some of the earlier missed subtle limitations and disadvantages in the positivistic approach. The dialogue also has led us to change and refine some of our opinions about how to construct useful knowledge.

A DIALECTICAL ANALYSIS

We find it helpful to use Hegel's dialectic to understand what is happening with regard to the scientific paradigms or basic assumptions that are currently used in family science—and in the social sciences generally. When the Hegelian dialectic is used to describe change, it assumes that at any time there is an ongoing three-step pattern in the way innovations and changes are made. The three-step pattern consists of a thesis, antithesis, and synthesis. The *thesis* is the status quo at any particular time. When any particular thesis is generally accepted as the normal way to think or behave, then there tends to be considerable consensus and little conflict. The *antithesis* is a reaction to the thesis that introduces ideas or patterns that are different from or in conflict with the thesis. When an antithesis is introduced in a community, it begins or accelerates controversy, conflict, debate, dialogue, and so on. The *synthesis* is a new way of thinking that tends to gradually emerge from the dialogue. Usually it is different from both the thesis and antithesis. It tends to have elements of both, although they are integrated in a unique way. Also, some new ideas may be introduced in the synthesis. The synthesis often becomes a widely accepted point of view, and as consensus develops it becomes a thesis in future changes.

The Thesis

The first step in our dialectical analysis is to identify the point of view that has been so widely shared that it can be viewed as a thesis. This paradigm can be described in several different ways. Some have called it the *Cartesian-Newtonian paradigm* (Capra, 1982). Brown and Paolucci (1979) called it *analytic-empirical science.* Some scholars call it *positivism* (Neuman, 1991). In Habermas's (1972) analysis, he calls it the *instrumental-technical paradigm.*

Morgaine recently summarized the main assumptions in this perspective as follows:

The [instrumental-technical paradigm] evolved from the natural sciences and addresses human interests concerned with satisfying the needs and wants related to shaping and controlling one's environment. This paradigm assumes that: (a) There is a single reality of life that is independent of human uniqueness; (b) the laws of human behavior are able to be discovered (through research); and (c) human needs can be satisfied by predicting cause and effect relationships and controlling human actions. (Morgaine, 1992, p. 12)

Critics have attributed several other assumptions to positivism. Positivists themselves had added another: Certainty is desirable and possible. As Williams and Olson point out, "The ultimate goal of positivism, empiricism, and structuralism is certainty about causal necessity (see Faulconer & Williams, 1985)" (1989, p. x).

Another assumption is that objectivity is possible and desirable. Human values, ethics, ideals, and goals are helpful in selecting research questions and in applying knowledge, but scholars are to try to be as objective as possible and not let their values intrude on the discovery and justification of knowledge.

Table 2.1 summarizes many of the main differences between positivism and the other scientific perspectives that are discussed in this chapter. The middle column on the left-hand page summarizes the main assumptions and goals in positivism. We are indebted to several scholars who have developed similar summaries in earlier literature, and we have incorporated many of their ideas in our summary (Brown & Paolucci, 1979; Coomer & Hultgren, 1989; Neuman, 1991).

One difference between the earlier descriptions of positivism and ours is that we have tried to maintain a balance between the rational and empirical aspects. Many earlier descriptions tended to overemphasize the empirical and underemphasize the rational features of positivism. When philosophers first began to describe positivism, they called it *logical positivism*, which is a more descriptive and accurate label.

The term *logical positivism* is more widely used, although *logical empiricism* is rapidly gaining in usage. Members of this

(continued on page 18)

Table 2.1 The Dialectical Analysis of Scientific Paradigms

	Thesis	Antitheses			Synthesis
	Positivism	*Interpretive Science*	*Critical-Emancipatory Approach*	*Ecosystems Approach*	
1. What are the ultimate objectives in scientific inquiry?	Universal generalizations can be produced that are explanatory in nature, laws of cause and effect can be identified, and prediction and control can be facilitated.	The subjective perceptions of meaning and interpretation can be understood.	Identify inequities and exploitation and help people become emancipated from them.	Gain knowledge that can be used to help individuals and families interact more effectively with their environments' goals.	Construct ideas that can be used to help families attain their goals. It is not useful to search for explanatory laws of cause and effect that would give prediction and control. The most valuable ideas are *general principles*.
2. What assumptions are held about causal laws?	Deterministic processes can be described with causal laws.	People may believe in causal laws, but it is the beliefs that are important, not the laws.	Causality is important, but it is not helpful to try to find causal laws. Each inequitable situation is unique.	Scholars who use this perspective believe in equifinality, which is the idea that many things can cause any outcome in human systems. The search for laws is irrational.	Equifinality exists, so the search for causal laws is irrelevant. Descriptive information and hypothetical, stochastic, phenomenal, and general principles that are *if-then* in nature are useful.

3. What are the key ontological assumptions (beliefs about the nature of reality)?	Things and processes exist independently of human knowledge of them. In Kantian terms, there is *noumena*.	Reality is subjective and fluid, and as many realities exist as people.	Conflict, inequity, power, and exploitation exist even if people are not aware of them. They can be overcome.	The various parts of reality are interconnected in important and systemic ways.	Noumena and phenomena both exist. All knowledge is phenomenal. Phenomenal beliefs are attempts to understand external and subjective realities.
4. What aspects of reality are important? (Which parts are studied?)	The focus is on parts that can be included in abstract theories and where empirical verification (observation with five senses) is possible.	The focus is on parts that have mental or cognitive interpretations, meanings, or definitions.	The focus is on inequities and underlying structures that maintain inequities and exploitation. Ideas and strategies can promote emancipation.	The focus is on the patterns in the processes in the near environment in which humans live. Considerable emphasis also is placed on values and choices that humans can make.	The focus is on parts that can be changed by individuals and families that will help them better attain their goals and ideals. The parts focused on most are the *patterns in the processes* in family systems.
5. How is reality known?	Reasoning constructs abstract theories, and empirical observation verifies the theories.	Subjective ideas are shared about the meaning of experience and the interpretations that individuals give their experience.	Critical inquiry is done into established ideas and social structures that promote inequities, and ideas are shared that promote awareness and change.	Reasoning and observation are used to try to identify the holistic patterns in interconnected systems.	A combination of rational and empirical methods is effective. Many different types of evidence can influence the amount of confidence we have in our scientific ideas.

Table 2.1 Continued

	Thesis		Antitheses		Synthesis
	Positivism	Interpretive Science	Critical-Emancipatory Approach	Ecosystems Approach	
6. What kinds of evidence are sought?	Empirical observations are made that others can repeat.	Subjective perceptions and definitions provide all necessary evidence.	Any kind of evidence can provide information on inequities, help increase consciousness, and evaluate the extent of emancipation.	Rational, observational, and clinical evidence are all valued.	A wide range of evidence is used, including clinical experience, reasoning, intuition, empirical observation, and subjective reports.
7. How is objectivity viewed?	Objectivity is possible; it is important to be as objective as possible in testing hypotheses.	Objectivity is usually viewed as either unimportant or impossible.	Objectivity and subjectivity are both important, but people often do not see the objective reality of their exploitation.	Objectivity and subjectivity are both important.	Objectivity and subjectivity are both important. Interpersonal corroboration is important in determining the confidence we should have in general principles.

8. How is certainty viewed?	Certainty *is* possible in testing causal laws.	Many realities exist, and certainty is always subjective.	Certainty about the existence and undesirability of inequities is assumed; seeking certainty about ideas is irrelevant.	Not a relevant issue; if an idea seems helpful, then it is used.	Certainty is neither possible nor sought with concepts, descriptions, and principles; these are merely phenomenal constructions that are intellectual tools; at best, they only approximate noumenal reality.
9. Where do values fit?	Science is value-neutral; values have no place except when topics are chosen or scientifically derived ideas are applied. The application of scientific ideas is not a part of science.	Values are an integral part of human experience and a main part of what is studied. Because values are subjective constructions, they do not have any absolute value, and no group's values are wrong, only different.	All science has value positions. Some positions are less desirable because they promote the status quo. Good value positions in science are always political and activist-oriented in trying to emancipate.	Values are important because they are an important part of systems and system interaction. Decision making is strongly emphasized in interacting with the environment; values have a central role in this interaction.	Values are an integral part of every aspect of scientific inquiry. They are important as subject matter because they determine the goals people and families seek. The values of scientists influence everything they do.

Table 2.1 Continued

| | Thesis | | Antitheses | | |
	Positivism	Interpretive Science	Critical-Emancipatory Approach	Ecosystems Approach	Synthesis
10. How important is action? If it is important, what is its role?	Action is not a central part of science. The goal is to construct laws of cause and effect that others can use.	Action is not central. The goals are to gain insights and understand interpretations.	Action is most central. Political action and social movements are valued.	Action is important: The goal of inquiry is to learn ideas that can be used in educational and therapeutic settings to help improve the quality of life.	Action is important. General principles provide the intellectual basis for intervention strategies that are designed to help families better attain their goals.
11. What role does common sense play?	Causal laws may become part of common sense, but common sense is of little value in discovering and justifying causal laws.	Powerful everyday theories are used by ordinary people. Common sense is as valid and as useful as scientific methods.	Common sense is suspect, and critical analysis is helpful. Common sense often leads to false beliefs that hide power and objective conditions.	Common sense is generally ignored as a source of scientific ideas or in gaining confidence in the ideas.	Common sense is important in managing family life and in identifying goals and ideals. Common sense is not an important part of scientific inquiry, but general principles can augment, help, and enrich common sense.

12. What is the nature of the human condition? How can scholarly inquiry improve it?	Humans live in a universe that is governed by laws; as they discover these governing laws, the quality of their lives improves.	Humans live in spontaneously evolving interaction with their social and physical environments; as they share meanings and interpretations, life is moral, humane, rich, and meaningful.	Humans live in inequity; powerful political and social conditions exploit and constrain. Criticism of established orders and constraining conditions can lead to emancipation.	Humans live in a complex set of enmeshed and interacting systems; understanding the ecological relationships helps humans make informed and wiser choices.	Life has opportunities and challenges, and people have ideals, values, goals, and resources they manage to attain their goals. General principles constructed by scholarly inquiry can help families better attain their goals.

school much prefer the latter term. They argue that "positivism" more accurately describes the early, crude and extremist days of the movement, rather than its current emphases. (Mead, 1953, p. 249)

The term *logical* denotes a marriage of rational and empirical epistemological processes. The development of theories and hypotheses is primarily a rational process, and it is important that we not exclude these rational aspects of this paradigm.

The Antitheses

There is a complication in our dialectical analysis as we try to identify "the" antithesis. The complication is that more than one perspective has been developed in opposition or as a reaction to positivism. There have been several different paradigmatic approaches, so it is more appropriate to refer to "antitheses."

Three alternatives to positivism have become important parts of the dialogue about how to do family science: the interpretive approach, a critical-emancipatory approach, and an ecosystemic approach. Their advocates each believe they are so different that they are unique paradigms in the sense that Kuhn (1970) has used this term.

The Interpretive Paradigm

This alternative has been described with several labels. Some call it an interpretive science (Brown & Paolucci, 1979), some an interpretive *paradigm* (Morgaine, 1992). Others call it *hermeneutics* (Thomas & Wilcox, 1987; Williams & Olson, 1989). We prefer the term *interpretive* because it is more general and inclusive.

Again, Morgaine's recent summary of the main assumptions in the interpretive paradigm is useful:

Assumptions underlying this paradigm include: (a) Natural science methods are not always appropriate for gaining insight into human interaction; (b) many human actions cannot be predicted or controlled; (c) attempts to manipulate and control others are not ethical; (d) there is no single reality of life—knowledge is created by individuals living in an historical era; [and] (e) gaining understanding or reflecting on meaning will serve as a catalyst for action. (Morgaine, 1992, p. 13)

Thus this point of view does not believe in certainty, law seeking, or objectivity. The objectives of the scholarly inquiry are to develop a conceptual framework, create a "universe of discourse" that provides insights, communicate about specific events that have meaning, and have conversations about the interpretations and meanings people have.

At least three different approaches use an interpretive orientation: symbolic interaction (not including the role theory branch of the interactionist approach), phenemonology, and hermeneutics.

Symbolic interaction was developed by George Herbert Mead, who believed the positivistic ideas developed by Pavlov and Watson in the behavioral school of thought are not very valuable in understanding humans. He believed that the higher mental processes of choice, value, meaning, ethical reasoning, interpretation, perception, and definition could not be understood with the behavioral approach. Those who have continued to develop the interactionist school of thought believe that what makes humans unique is creating meaning by "defining the objects, events, and situations which they encounter" (Blumer, 1962, p. 686).

The interactionist school of thought has been one of the major theoretical approaches in the field for decades. Every review of the conceptual frameworks or theories that are used in the family field has given this perspective center stage (Boss, Doherty, LaRossa, & Schumm, 1992; Broderick, 1971; Burr, Jensen, & Brady, 1977; Christensen, 1964; Hill & Hansen, 1960; Holman & Burr, 1980; Nye & Berardo, 1966).

A second approach that uses the interpretive paradigm is the *phenomonological school* of thought described by McLain and Weigert (1979). It builds on the philosophical writings of scholars such as Schutz (1967, 1970). It focuses on constructing meaning about the activities of everyday life. This approach has not yet been widely adopted by family scholars.

A third approach is *hermeneutics*. The scholars who prefer this method of constructing knowledge build on the work of philosophers such as Heidegger (1962). This is a relatively new perspective in the family field; it was not even mentioned until the late 1970s and early 1980s.

The three approaches that use an interpretive paradigm have several differences. Symbolic interactionists assume it is useful to identify a conceptual framework that is general and abstract. Some of the scholars who like the hermeneutic approach seem to assume that attention should be given primarily to specific and situational interpretations, narratives, and conversations rather than general or abstract ideas (Hultgren, 1989). They seem to believe that when generalizations are made, it dehumanizes the insights. This is a radical departure from scholarship in the sciences, arts, and humanities, and we suspect this part of the hermeneutic approach will be short-lived. Table 2.1 also summarizes the main assumptions and goals in the interpretive paradigm.

The Critical or Emancipatory Paradigm

The critical or emancipatory approach is a second reaction to positivism. There are, of course, other reasons for this perspective, but its popularity in the last few decades has been partly because it is an alternative to positivism. The primary goals in this approach are to raise the consciousness of people about oppression and to help emancipate oppressed people from subjugation. This primary goal is quite different from the goals of acquiring scientific laws or focusing on interpretive processes to create new knowledge.

There is a long tradition of scholarship about the evils of domination and exploitation and the value of personal autonomy, justice, and freedom. Rousseau's (1750, 1762) writings on these issues helped spawn political revolutions in the United States and France in the 18th century, and his writings also helped equality and freedom become ideals that many believe are important. Several groups of scholars believe these ideals are compromised in many ways in society, and they are dedicated to developing ideas and strategies that are critical of existing orders and that emancipate those who are oppressed.

Some of these scholars have focused on political oppression. They tend to take an activist approach to developing ideas that will help emancipate people from oppressive governments (Fromm, 1941; Habermas, 1972, 1981).

A different group of scholars has focused on the plight of women, and they have developed a new field called *feminism*. They believe women to be oppressed (Walker, Martin, & Thompson, 1988), and they have developed a large body of literature that is critical of the established order. The scholars who use this perspective have demonstrated serious and unrecognized gender biases in previously accepted theories, research, and practices in many fields of inquiry (Gilligan, 1982), and their arguments are so persuasive that they are literally revolutionizing academia.

Some of the critical-emancipatory paradigm's assumptions are the same as those in the interpretive paradigm. For example, both paradigms assume the first four beliefs mentioned above for the interpretive perspective. In addition, the critical-emancipatory approach assumes that the personal experiences of being oppressor and oppressed are political, whether or not people recognize it; it is ethical to actively work toward emancipation; a wide range of ideas and methods that promote emancipation should be used; and the positivistic approach is harmful when it is used to distance people from the emancipatory struggles and to promote the status quo—as it frequently is. Table 2.1 also summarizes some of this approach's main assumptions.

Ecosystemic Approach

A third reaction to positivism has become an important part of family science. It is part of a larger movement that is known as a *systemic* or *ecosystemic approach* (Capra, 1982; Doherty, 1986). The family science version of this approach was developed first by several different groups of scholars who apparently worked quite independently of one another. One group was at the Mental Research Institute in Palo Alto in the 1950s and included Gregory Bateson, Richard Jackson, and Paul Watzlawick. Their philosophical ideas were first articulated by Watzlawick, Beavin, and Jackson (1967) and Bateson (1972, 1979). These ideas were later expanded by others such as Keeney and Sprenkle (1982) and Auerswald (1985, 1987).

Another group of scholars was in home economics. Their version of these ideas was developed primarily by Beatrice Paolucci (Paolucci, Hall, & Axinn, 1977), but many others also have made important contributions (Deacon & Firebaugh, 1986; Gross, Crandall, & Knoll, 1980). A third group of family-oriented scholars who use an ecological approach was in developmental psychology. This group tried to move developmental psychology away from an overdependence on laboratory work and toward closely examining the contexts in which children develop (Bronfenbrenner, 1979; Garbarino, 1982). This group, however, has not been as consistent as a reaction to positivism.

There are several common denominators in these groups. They all emphasize familial processes as fundamental and unique, and they used an ecosystemic approach. At the assumptive level, they assumed the following:

1. Humans have higher mental and ethical processes such as thinking, choosing, meaning, valuing, and having goals, and it is important to focus on these parts of the human experience.
2. It is important to be relatively holistic.
3. It is helpful to think in systemic terms to capture the interactions between humans and their different environments and their subsystems.
4. Patterns in processes are the phenomena that yield the most useful information.
5. It is helpful to focus on ways of intervening in on-going systems to help them attain their goals rather than seek law-like statements about cause and effect.

Table 2.1 also summarizes some of the main assumptions and goals in the systemic perspective.

When we think of the systemic perspective as a paradigmatic shift (Keeney & Sprenkle, 1982), it is important that we realize that this is quite different from general systems theory. General systems theory is a fairly positivistic attempt to identify aspects of systems that are universal or common to all systems. The general systems perspective constructed several concepts that have been adopted by the nonpositivistic, family-oriented systems scholars, but the basic assumptions are quite different.

We find one aspect of this dialectical analysis intriguing. We are puzzled by why the previous descriptions of the paradigms that are used in the family field have not included the ecosystemic approach as a separate reaction to positivism (Brown & Paolucci, 1979; Morgaine, 1992; Neuman, 1991; Thomas & Wilcox, 1987). These earlier descriptions included the interpretive and critical alternatives, but none included the ecosystemic alternative. It seems to us obvious that the ecosystemic epistemology is a reactionary point of view and that it is quite different from the interpretive and critical approaches. Yet it has not been viewed this way in any of the earlier analyses. Another aspect of these reactionary approaches that makes this omission doubly puzzling is that the hermeneutic approach has not yet developed any new substantive ideas. It still remains a way of thinking that we hope will contribute new ideas. At the same time, the systemic approach has contributed a large number of concepts and propositions that many family scientists have found useful.

A Synthesis

We believe the family field in particular and the social sciences in general are moving into a new phase in the nature of the paradigms that are used. The new phase will be an era in which an increasing number of family scholars will use syntheses of earlier perspectives.

Undoubtedly, we will continue to have positivism, and a large number of the scholars in the family field will continue to prefer this approach. We also will probably continue to have all three of the reactions to positivism, and some scholars will prefer to use these approaches in their "pure" form.

We also suspect there will be different approaches in the synthesis phase of the dialectical change. We are using one particular synthesis in this volume, but we suspect other syntheses will appear. The main assumptions we use in our synthesis are described below and summarized in Table 2.1.

Our ultimate objectives come primarily from the critical-emancipatory and ecosystemic approaches. Our objectives are activist in nature: We are trying to construct ideas that can be used by practitioners such as educators and therapists to help family members attain their individual and collective goals. Our progress toward obtaining these objectives is guided by several important assumptions. Because these assumptions guide our thinking, research, and outcomes, we believe it is helpful to expose our assumptions both for our benefit and others who are interested in this work.

One important assumption is our belief in equifinality and equipotentiality. These concepts suggest that it is impossible to have one-to-one causal laws in complex systems such as families. We thus do not believe it is useful to search for explanations or explanatory laws of cause and effect that would give prediction and control. An implication of this assumption is that we are not interested in research that tries to find determinants, account for variance, or seek causes. Incidentally, we are aware that this assumption means that we are in a minority and out of the mainstream of the social sciences.

With regard to ontological assumptions, we share the positivistic idea that things exist independently of human knowledge about them. Kant referred to these realities as *noumena,* and part of our goal is to gain more knowledge about noumena that will enable us to help families better attain their goals. Human knowledge of noumena, however, is always constructed, phenomenal, and subjective, and different perceptions are different views of reality. There also is a great deal of human knowledge about family processes that do not deal with noumena. It is entirely phenomenal, and part of our goal is to better understand this phenomenal knowledge and the role it has in family processes. The various parts of reality are, of course, interconnected in complex ecological networks, and so we believe it is important to emphasize an ecological or context-sensitive approach to gaining and using knowledge.

The parts of reality on which we focus are those that we think will help us and others assist families to lead more satisfying lives. The parts we focus on the most are the patterns in the processes in family systems, the environmental systems around families, and the subsystems inside families. Some areas that seem the most relevant to us are emotional and developmental processes, interpretations, loving, meanings, inequities, underlying structures, values, choices, and generational connections.

We assume that many different methods can be used to construct knowledge. We rely primarily on the combination of rational and empirical methods that has been developed in the positivistic tradition, but we view these methods broadly. For example, we believe there are many different types of evidence that should influence the amount of confidence we have in our scientific ideas. Empirical evidence from surveys and experiments is valuable. Clinical evidence also is useful, as is rational evidence, which can be acquired by connecting ideas with other well-established ideas or by providing a rationale. Also, in many situations an intuitive basis can be persuasive. For example, we do not know of one empirical study, published clinical evidence, or even published attempts to develop a rationale for the principle of least interest other than Waller's (1938) initial formulation, but most family scientists seem to have considerable confidence in it.

We believe objectivity is impossible in an ultimate sense. We humans live our lives phenomenally and subjectively, and we cannot escape this reality. On the other hand, part of what the positivists were trying to do with what they called *objectivity* is valuable, and we believe it ought to be retained. This objectivity is to try to find corroboration in the search for evidence for and against our scientific ideas. It is much more persuasive to have the work of several different research teams provide cumulative and corroborative evidence about the usefulness of our ideas. This is especially the case when research teams do not have a personal investment in the ideas that are being tested. We believe that it is only through interpersonal corroboration that we can acquire much evidence about scientific ideas. Each individual is always subjective, but when a community of scholars shares its subjective experiences about the evidence for and against scholarly ideas, it justifies a weight of evidence that is helpful in making judgments about which ideas to retain, modify, and eliminate from our theories.

We also assume it desirable to have *cumulativity* in our scientific ideas. We have observed with some dismay that relatively little cumulativity has occurred in the social sciences in the 20th century.

Most social scientists seem to think that an idea that is a few decades old is not useful, and thus they look for a new guru who will provide a new approach. It may be that this is partly because our paradigms are not yet very effective. We remain optimistic that we will have more cumulativity in the future than in the past, even though there always will be an evolving metamorphosis in our ideas as cultures and issues change.

We assume that generalization is desirable. This means we do not share the idea advocated by some critics of positivism that scientific ideas should not rise above shared narrations and conversations about specific lived events (Hultgren, 1989). Sharing specific experiences is useful for the individuals involved, and this is a vehicle that can be helpful in learning scientific ideas and finding ways to apply our generalizations. However, if ideas never rise above narrations and conversations about specifics, then they will remain so idiosyncratic that they will be of little value to a community of scholars and practitioners. We believe it is the body of shared and continually evolving abstract generalizations that are socially constructed that is the most valuable payoff in the scientific method.

We assume there are at least three different kinds of generalizations that are useful. One is *descriptive* generalizations, which are descriptions of patterns in the processes in family systems. They describe *what* is happening, but they do not give us information about why or how to intervene to make things better.

The other two kinds of generalizations both deal with patterns of covariation among variables or processes. One kind of these covariational generalizations is the most valuable of the three to us: *general principles* (Burr, 1976; Burr, Jensen, & Brady, 1977). These are general statements that have a certain type of *if-then* quality to them. The "if" part refers to aspects of family processes where intervention is possible. This part is typically called the *independent* variable in the positivistic paradigm. In our synthesis of the paradigms, we are sensitive to the idea that nothing is "independent," so we do not think about independent variables. We change what we emphasize or think about and focus on system processes where intervention is possible. The "then" part refers to outcomes that we think tend to occur in fairly predictable ways.

The third kind of generalization that is used in the field is the type that identifies covariation but with no basis for intervention. Most of the complex statistical analyses in current journals are of this type. They give us information about the covariation of variables, and they often tell us about the accounted for proportion of "variance," but they do not provide a basis for intervention. The difference between the second and third type of generalization is subtle but important for those of us who are interested in an activist type of knowledge. We have little interest in this third type of generalization.

We believe there are deterministic processes at work with regard to some aspects of family systems. For example, many biological processes operate with deterministic processes—for example, genetics and hormonal changes. Also, some indeterministic processes work with some aspects of family systems. At the level of sophistication we have in the 1990s, we do not understand much about when determinism and indeterminism occur. Therefore, most of the time, when we are dealing with social processes, the best we can do is to think with probabilities. Thus with our best general principles all we can do is believe that *if* certain interventions are made, it *tends to* change the probability of various outcomes. Thus we believe the search for causality and the search for certainty in scientific ideas are futile. Our best scientific ideas tell us little about what actually causes what, and they are always tentative and subject to revision and modification in the light of new theories, concepts, and empirical data.

The research reported in this book does not attempt to discover general principles. We wish it did, but the findings are still too preliminary. This project is primarily a descriptive project that is laying the groundwork for the future development of principles about how families can cope effectively with stress.

We believe values have a place in all aspects of scientific inquiry. They help us decide what to study, how to study, how to do our research in humane and effective ways, and how to use the ideas we develop. It is because we value families that we focus on them. We believe that when we are wise in the familial part of our lives, then our family experiences can help us have rich and rewarding experiences. Our goals are to help discover ideas that will help us all be more effective in creating healthy and strong families.

We appreciate the way the critical-emancipatory paradigm has sensitized us to many issues and processes, and we share the activist orientation of this approach. Our agenda includes gender issues, but it also includes many other difficulties, tragedies, and serious problems in the family realm that we think also deserve attention. For example, we believe that conditions in the family realm are the most basic taproots for the substance abuse and crime problems that receive so much attention in our society. We also believe that public-realm approaches such as changing our legal, police, military, and educational systems will do little to alleviate these problems.

The public-realm attempts to cope with these problems are like trying to change the spots of measles by putting salve on them or incarcerating people who have spots. We believe we would be more effective in helping solve our problems if we changed our approach and tried to create an ecology where different forms of family life and human behavior thrive. In addition to general feminist issues, other broad familial issues also deserve attention such as the tragedies of unsupportiveness, lack of understanding, closeness avoidance, insensitivity, and cycles of violence. Our energies are devoted to discovering ideas that can be used to improve many different aspects of family life.

A second contribution we appreciate from the feminist literature is that, as scholars such as Gouldner (1988) have argued, gender issues ought to be a central concern in family science. This assumption has led us to pay attention to gender issues and processes in several different ways in each chapter of this book.

SUMMARY

This chapter identifies the paradigm that guided this project. To identify our assumptions, we have done a dialectical analysis of the major paradigms within the field. We suggest that the positivistic paradigm can be viewed as a thesis and that the various criticisms of positivism can be viewed as antitheses. Most of the descriptions of the paradigmatic orientations that are used in the family field suggest two major alternatives to positivism: interpretive and critical-emancipatory approaches. We suggest that the ecosystemic perspective is a third reaction to positivism, and we observed that our paradigmatic approach uses some of the assumptions in each of these approaches but is not adequately described by any of them. Therefore, we have tried to describe a synthesis that benefits from many of the useful aspects of each. The last part of this chapter is an attempt to summarize the main assumptions in our approach and describe how these assumptions are played out in the later chapters. Our attempt to identify a synthesized approach does not suggest that this will eliminate the other approaches. Quite the contrary. Each of the various paradigms will undoubtedly continue to have its advocates. Thus what we have is a condition that is increasingly pluralistic in terms of the paradigmatic orientations that are used in the field. We believe that the synthesis describes an orientation that is used by many of the more intervention-minded theorists, researchers, and practitioners in the family field, especially family life educators and family therapists.

The study of family stress has been dominated by a positivistic orientation, and we hope this project will help move this area of inquiry in the direction of being a search for general principles that can help families cope more effectively with stress.

THREE

A Systems Model of Family Stress

The ABC-X models have been the dominant family stress theory for almost half a century (Boss, 1987, 1988; Christensen, 1964). These models have been and undoubtedly will continue to be useful in several ways. However, the ABC-X models also have several limitations and disadvantages that limit their usefulness. The limitations derive from (a) the positivistic assumptions that underlie the models and (b) inconsistencies in the assumptions used in the models.

We believe the solution to these limitations is to separate the ABC-X models from the systemic ideas that have been constructed in the last several decades by scholars such as Hamilton McCubbin and Pauline Boss. The separation results in two theories rather than one, and both are more internally consistent, testable, and useful by separation. The separation was initially proposed by Robert Burr (1989), and he demonstrated how the separation allowed him to develop several new theoretical ideas in the systems theory of family stress.

The purpose of this chapter is first to describe Burr's theoretical innovations and second to explain how his ideas were used in the current project to develop several testable hypotheses. Some of these hypotheses are then empirically tested, and some are subsequently revised and extended in the later chapters of this book.

A SHORT HISTORY OF FAMILY STRESS THEORY

Research about family stress began in the 1930s (Angell, 1936; Cavan & Ranck, 1938; Komorovsky, 1940). Hill (1949) built systematically on these initial studies in his benchmark study of postwar family stress in which he developed his ABC-X model. These initial studies set the theoretical agenda and research standards that have dominated the literature about family stress. As several scholars have argued in recent years (Boss, 1988; Walker, 1985), the basic assumptions and goals in these studies were guided by the scientific paradigm that is currently known as logical positivism (Capra, 1982; Doherty, 1986).

The ABC-X model is fundamentally a positivistic theory because its purpose is to identify causal relationships that specify deterministic patterns. The A, B, and C factors combine to cause or determine the X, or the amount of crisis in families. This model assumes that the variables operate in a relatively mechanistic, linear, and cause-and-effect manner.

The 1960s and 1970s saw a rapid growth in the understanding and usefulness of this approach to family stress (Burr, 1973; Hansen & Hill, 1964; Hansen & Johnson, 1979; Hill, 1958). However, this growth remained fundamentally within the framework of the ABC-X model and its positivistic assumptions.

In the last two decades several scholars have tried to break out of some of the limitations of the ABC-X model by making it more systemic and finding ways to make it more consistent with non-positivistic ways of thinking. For example, Boss (1975, 1977) introduced the concept of *boundary ambiguity*. McCubbin and Patterson (1982) introduced the idea of *feedback loops* to try to correct the problem of linearity. The concept of *coping strategies* (McCubbin, 1979) was introduced to include other systemic processes.

These innovations improved the ABC-X model. However, they also introduced a complication that has now become a serious problem. The addition of these systemic factors assumes that fundamental positivistic assumptions are made when we think about the systemic processes and the A, B, C, and X factors. Although some of the intellectual traditions in systems theory are indeed positivistic (Buckley, 1968), the family-oriented systems theories developed by scholars such as Bateson (1972), Bowen (Kerr & Bowen, 1988), Paolucci et al. (1977), Keeney and Sprenkle (1982), and Auerswald (1987) have a set of assumptions that are fundamentally different. These family theorists have a set of presuppositions that are part of a nonpositivistic scientific paradigm (Becvar & Becvar, 1988; Doherty, 1986; Kuhn, 1970).

It is also our thesis that the systemic ideas about family stress that have been introduced in the last two decades are fundamentally part of this nonpositivistic approach. The result is that, even though the newer ABC-X models were introduced in an attempt to improve the older models and they make important new contributions, they have serious inconsistencies at the assumptive level. These inconsistencies have profound implications for theorists who try to add to the models, researchers who try to test the resulting models, and practitioners who try to use these ideas as the basis for intervention.

Our intent is not to undermine or replace the ABC-X model, but to suggest that now is time to separate the more linear, deterministic, causal ABC-X ideas from the nonlinear, indeterministic, systemic family stress model. By doing this, the resulting models are more valuable. They are more heuristic: Several new research questions are raised. They are theoretically more fruitful because several new theoretical insights can be generated that are not apparent when the two theoretical models are combined. They are more valuable in a practical sense because the new ideas have important implications for practitioners.

THEORIZING ABOUT FAMILY STRESS

Family Stress as Process

To begin, the term stress needs a systems-type definition. The best way to do this is to define stress as a process that is interrelated with several other processes in the system. One way to conceptualize these processes is to begin by describing several processes that occur in family systems when they are not in stressful situations.

When family systems are not experiencing stress, there is a fairly predictable repetition or redundancy in the patterns of the daily routines and events. The family members interact with little difficulty, and the family systems are involved in processes of transforming inputs into outputs with relative ease. As Kantor and Lehr (1975) pointed out, families transform inputs such as energy, time, and space into outputs such as meaning, affection, and power. Other inputs include behaviors, money, and information. Other outputs include love, attention, discipline, growth, development, satisfaction, bonds, heritage, closeness, learning, and security (Gross et al., 1980; Paolucci et al., 1977).

To carry out these transformation processes, families develop a large number of rules, sometimes called *rules of transformation* (Broderick & Smith, 1979). These rules govern the hourly, daily, and weekly routines and cycles of life. Some of the rules are explicit, but most are implicit understandings (Reiss, 1981). Family systems continually monitor the negative and positive feedback to see if the outputs are within the agreed-upon standards or limits the family has set (Gross et al., 1980; Paolucci et al., 1977).

Developmental changes and unexpected changes constantly create some change (morphogenesis) in family systems, but during relatively calm periods the morphogenetic tendencies are moderated by morphostatic tendencies. The result is that systems have manageable levels of change and order, innovation and constancy, and creativity and predictability. There is a continual balancing and rebalancing of the needs people have for togetherness and separateness (Kerr & Bowen, 1988, chap. 3), and the system is always responding to generational, emotional, affective, economic, social, and ecological factors both outside and inside the family.

Even during rare times when family systems are able to settle down to "normal," the systems are an evolving and dynamic flow of energy, resources, activity, tensions, agreements, diversity, consensus, loving, anger, new information, and old and new traditions. Also, there is always a changing composition of age, gender, involvement, distance regulation, and interaction with the environmental systems (Hoffman, 1981).

As families evolve through time, they develop what systems theorists call a *requisite variety of rules of transformation*. This means they develop enough rules about how things should be done that they are able to transform the inputs into outputs in ways that comfortably meet minimal standards in attaining individual and family goals.

Family stress occurs when feedback indicates the system does not have the requisite variety of rules to transform comfortably inputs into outputs that meet desirable standards. In other words, the process of stress occurs when the usual transformation processes are not sufficient for families to handle a change or new input in the system. For example, if a new infant is born and the family has the requisite variety of rules to cope with the new member, then the family does not experience stress. However, if the family does not have the requisite variety of rules to cope, then it tends to have difficultly dealing with this input, which is stressful for the system.

When stress occurs, it interferes with the normal transformation processes. Rather than engaging in their usual and preferred activities, families find themselves asking "What are we going to do?" and "How are we going to deal with this situation?" Some of the outward manifestations of this systemic stress are that meals may not get fixed and cleaned up in the usual way, other daily routines are disrupted, tension tends to increase, rituals are not performed in the usual manner, attention is diverted to the stressful situation, and normally desired interactions with the environment are disrupted.

Developmental Patterns

Koos (1946) developed a roller-coaster model that is helpful in conceptualizing some of the developmental aspects of family stress. The model refers to changes in the patterns in a family system, so it is an essential part of a systemic theory of family stress. The version of the roller-coaster model we used in this project is shown in Figure 3.1.

The model consists of a series of fairly predictable developmental transitions and stages. The horizontal line at far left represents

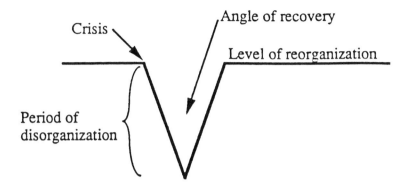

Figure 3.1 The Koos Roller-Coaster Model of Family Stress

the first stage. It shows the quality of a family's functioning when it is in a normal state or before it experiences a particular stressful situation. This part of the model was labeled the *pretrauma phase* by Boss (1987).

According to the Koos model, the stressor event is an input that precipitates a transition into a second stage. The second stage is the first of two coping stages. It was called the *acute coping phase* by McCubbin and Dahl (1985). According to Koos, this stage is a period of disorganization that is depicted by a drop in the line. He observed that some stressors lead to more disorganization than others; this is shown in the graph as the line drops lower in some situations than in others.

As time passes, according to the Koos model, families eventually experience another transition. When the disorganization reaches this lowest point, the family moves into the third developmental stage or the *recovery period*. During this phase, families use a variety of coping strategies to try to manage the disruption introduced by the stressful situation. If the coping strategies do not readily adjust the family system so it can handle the stress, then there is a large *angle of recovery*, and the family may continue in a disrupted condition for a long period of time.

The next transition occurs at the end of the recovery period. It occurs when the deliberate coping ends and the families are past the recovery process. This transition begins the fourth and final developmental phase—a period that it is a new normal level of functioning for the system.

When we use a systems concept of family stress, we recognize that several of these roller-coaster patterns could be occurring simultaneously in an interacting and overlapping way. In addition, a family may be in different phases of the developmental pattern with regard to several different potentially stressful inputs.

Integrating the Systemic Concepts Developed Earlier

Several systemic concepts about family stress have been developed in the last two decades. These concepts have been developed by different groups of scholars, such as Boss (1975, 1977, 1987, 1988), McCubbin and his colleagues (McCubbin & Figley, 1983; McCubbin et al., 1980; McCubbin & Patterson, 1982, 1983), Reiss (1981), Pearlin and Schooler (1982), and Montgomery and Fewer (1988).[1] All of these previously developed concepts should be viewed as part of a systems theory of family stress. If these concepts had not been developed earlier, it would not be possible to put it all together now in a new and more internally consistent theory.

One such concept, *boundary ambiguity*, was introduced by Boss (1975, 1977). Boundary ambiguity refers to degree of uncertainty in a family's perception of who is and is not in the family, who operates in which roles and tasks in the family system, and how much openness there should be in allowing various inputs into the system. This concept has been found to be helpful in understanding and intervening in a wide range of stressful situations (Boss, 1988; Burns, 1985).

Thinking systemically about boundary issues helps us deal with several theoretical, empirical, and practical questions, such as the following:

1. What are the processes that families use or go through to develop boundary clarity?
2. What kind of coping strategies can change or improve unhealthy processes of clarifying boundaries?

3. What are the different aspects or parts of the process that can then be manipulated?
4. What other processes in the family system are influenced by having unclear boundaries?

McCubbin and Patterson (1982) introduced the concept of *stress pile-up*. This concept refers to experiencing simultaneous multiple stressor events and having new stressors occur before old ones are eliminated. McCubbin and Patterson (1982) studied the stressor event of fathers missing because of the Vietnam War and found that nonnormative stressors such as hardships inherent in the separation stressor, stress from the normal development of family members over time, and trial-and-error efforts to manage stressful situations accumulated over time. This pile-up increased the difficulty of the stress families had to handle.

Stress pile-up is a systemic concept, but it was introduced first as an addition to the double ABC-X model. When it is used as part of the ABC-X model, it limits the concept's usefulness. In the ABC-X model, the A, B, and C factors are added to create X, and stress pile-up does not come into play until after the X has occurred. Because of the deterministic, linear, and additive nature of the model, it does not lead to the conceptualization that stress can be introduced into family systems at any time and that different stressor events may occur simultaneously.

When we use the concept of stress pile-up as part of a systems model rather than as a part of the ABC-X model, it is a more useful. It is conceptualized as multiple inputs entering into the system. Because the stress processes are seen as ongoing with constant interaction and change, it is easy to conceptualize simultaneous processes such as multiple inputs at any time. When we think about pile-up in this way, it helps theorists, researchers, and practitioners realize that families who experience new stressor events before they have coped with earlier ones tend to be more troubled than if the old inputs had been adequately handled. The concept of stress pile-up also allows practitioners and scholars to understand that the normal or prestress stage in Figure 3.1 is rarely prestress. It is "pre-" only for a particular stressor that is a new input, and in most family systems several other stressors are already being managed.

Thus the stage in which families are is relative to which inputs and processes we are focusing on at a given moment.

Another useful concept—*coping strategies*—was introduced in the middle 1970s (Boss, McCubbin, & Lester, 1979; McCubbin, 1979; McCubbin, Dahl, Lester, Benson, & Robertson, 1976). The construction of this concept was an important contribution in several ways. It focused attention on the management process rather than on deterministic relationships, and it is a concept that has been very helpful to theorists, researchers, and practitioners.

The definition of the situation was the C part of the ABC-X model, and it is a helpful part of all ABC-X models. It also is possible to think about this concept systemically rather than deterministically. When we use this idea in a systems model, we do not care about how it contributes deterministically to the amount of crisis. What we care about are such things as how the definition influences several processes in the system. For example, we could be concerned with how the definition influences processes in the acute phase or the recovery phase if a family system has been disrupted. We also could be interested in how the family responds to the defining process itself and how that may have an effect on other family processes.

When the definition of the situation is viewed in this systemic manner, it becomes a dynamic and useful part of the systems theory. Research has shown that families tend to manage stressful situations more successfully when they are able to define the situations optimistically and proactively. Conversely, when a family has defined a situation in a pessimistic manner, the situation is more difficult to manage (McCubbin & Dahl, 1985). Chapters 6 and 7 in this book use these ideas in developing a more refined conceptual framework of management strategies than has existed previously in the family literature.

David Reiss (1981) introduced a different set of systems concepts into the family stress literature. He pointed out that the rules in families tend to change in different ways when families experience stress. When families are not experiencing stress, the rules tend to remain implicit, covert parts of the system, and they gradually evolve in ways that are generally out of the consciousness of family members. However, during periods of stress, the family rules tend to become more explicit. Families talk more about how they ought to be behaving, how they might change their rules, and how they could alter their patterns to help the system run more smoothly and help them be more effective.

Thus when a family finds it necessary to make implicit rules explicit, it is an indicator that the family is in trouble. This idea adds an additional dimension to the systems theory of stress by giving us new insights about what happens in families when they encounter and cope with difficult situations.

THEORETICAL QUESTIONS

When we use a systems theory instead of a positivistic theory, we ask fundamentally different questions about family stress. Researchers and others with a positivistic orientation use theory to frame questions such as the following:

- What causes the variation in the criterion variables?
- What are the explanatory variables?
- What explains the variance?
- How can we test the covariational relationships?
- How do we operationalize the variables?
- What are the causes?
- Where is the explanation of variation in the outcome variables?

The following paragraphs introduce questions generated from a systems viewpoint that we think are helpful. Some of these questions are then dealt with in the later chapters.

Different Developmental Patterns?

In Chapter 5, we will examine some of the questions that are important from a systems perspective and that deal with the nature of the developmental processes. Koos theorized that after the introduction of a stressor event into a family, all families developmentally moved into a period of disorganization. We believe, however, that several new theoretical questions should be asked about this idea.

Thinking systemically, it seems possible that some families may be able to cope with their stressful situations in ways that avoid a period of disorganization. Reiss also has questioned the simplicity of Koos's idea:

[I]n our view, stress, crisis, and disorganization in family life are almost never sequential links in an orderly chain of events. On the contrary, they interpenetrate one another, enhance, distort, reinforce, and mute each other in endless varieties of chain reactions and feedback loops in immediate sequences or after long periods of time. (Reiss, 1981, p. 176)

Thus it is possible that our previous thinking is too simplistic. It is possible that the Koos response pattern occurs in some circumstances but not in others. Also, it is possible that some families may improve their situations in life through coping processes and never enter into periods of disorganization when they encounter stressful situations.

These theoretical questions are addressed in Chapter 4. Brent Harker was the principle investigator for this chapter, and he examined our data to determine whether different developmental patterns existed in several unique situations; if so, his goal was to describe the other patterns. As we thought about this question and about how our own families had coped with various stressful situations, we theorized that the Koos pattern is not universal. We recalled situations in our own families where a stressful situation occurred, such as a death, and the family functioning became better and never experienced the decrease that Koos postulated.

Because the goal of this chapter is merely to articulate the theory that guided our inquiry and the theoretical questions in which we were interested, we are not presenting our findings about these questions here. The findings are presented in Chapter 4.

Do Different Aspects of Family Systems Respond Differently?

In Chapter 6, we examine what previous theorizing and research have not addressed: Do different parts of family systems tend to respond differently to stress? The systems theory raises the following theoretical and empirical question: Does the emotional system (Kerr & Bowen, 1988) tend to respond differently to family stress than the functioning of the leadership subsystem or communication? Or is it possible that in some situations parts of family systems tend to improve under stress while others tend to be disrupted? If this does occur, do these response patterns tend to be different for different kinds of stressful situations?

These questions have not, to our knowledge, been addressed in previous theorizing or research, but they seem to us to be important theoretical questions. Therefore, several members of our research team have addressed these questions in Chapter 5. Russell McClure and Alan Taylor analyzed our data to determine what the developmental response patterns are with regard to several different aspects of family systems. Specifically, they looked at the way the following nine aspects of the system:

1. changes in marital satisfaction,
2. changes in rituals and celebrations,
3. disruptions or improvements in daily routines and chores,
4. cohesion or togetherness in the family,
5. emotional climate,
6. quality of communication,
7. progression through the normal stages of family development,
8. executive subsystem (leadership and decision making), and
9. amount of contention present.

The Role of Coping Strategies

In Chapters 7 and 8 we will consider many important theoretical and empirical questions about the role of coping strategies in family stress. McCubbin and Figley (1983) reviewed the literature about coping strategies and identified 11 that they suggested are "universally" helpful and enabling when families encounter stress. Thus far, however, there is relatively little data on which to base this rather sweeping claim.

Also, the previous literature about coping strategies is relatively confusing. Different scholars have generated different lists of strategies, but there is little overlap among them. Some scholars pay attention to certain strategies and ignore others, and some use certain terms in quite different ways. We thus believe there is a need to examine the way we are conceptualizing coping strategies and to develop an integrated and synthesized conceptual framework. Two members of our research team, Paul Martin and Wesley Burr, address this task, and their analysis is in Chapter 7.

After Martin and Burr create their conceptual framework of coping strategies, we devote Chapter 8 to determining which coping strategies are widely or rarely used, which tend to be the most and least helpful, and which tend to be harmful. This chapter is written by Daniel Stuart and Paul Martin.

Does the Use of Coping Strategies Have a Sequence?

In Chapter 9, another set of systems-type questions deals with whether a sequence exists in the management strategies that families find helpful and useful. For example, are certain strategies helpful right after the stressor event appears and are others helpful at later stages in stress management? Robert Burr (1993) developed theoretical ideas that suggest such a sequence in the way families use certain coping strategies, and Chapter 9 is Cindy Doxey's analysis of our data to begin testing Burr's ideas. Burr's theoretical speculations are summarized in the next section of this chapter, and it is an illustration of another way in which the systems model of family stress can generate new theoretical ideas.

NEW THEORETICAL IDEAS

Having a systems theory of family stress has several advantages. It makes it possible to be indeterministic in our thinking. It also is possible to redefine concepts and integrate old ideas so that they are parts of a more coherent family stress theory. It allows us to redefine and use several old ideas in ways that are more useful. Also, as demonstrated in the preceding discussion, it helps generate several new research questions that deserve attention. Most important, however, it facilitates theory development in two additional ways. First, some existing systems theory ideas that have not been applied to family stress can now be integrated into the stress theory, and this makes the theory of family stress more comprehensive. Second, the more comprehensive theory provides the basis for several new theoretical ideas. The purpose of this section is to identify some of these new theoretical ideas.

The new insights were constructed by integrating two concepts that were previously developed in other systems theory literature and trying to use these concepts to understand stress processes. The two concepts are *levels of abstraction* (Burr, 1991; Sluzki, 1983; Watzlawick et al., 1974) and *family paradigms* (Constantine, 1986; Reiss, 1981). Before the new theoretical insights can be understood, these two concepts will be briefly explained.

Levels of Abstraction and Family Paradigms

Watzlawick and his colleagues (1974) used group theory and the theory of logical types to argue that systems can have two different levels of change.

> Group theory gives us a framework for thinking about the kind of change that can occur within a system that itself stays invariant; the theory of logical types is not concerned with what goes on inside a class, i.e., between its members, but gives us a frame for considering the relationship between member and class and the peculiar metamorphosis which is in the nature of shifts from one logical level to the next higher. If we accept this basic distinction between the two theories, it follows that there are two different types of change: one that occurs within a given system which itself remains unchanged, and one whose occurrence changes the system itself. To exemplify this distinction in more behavioral terms: a person having a nightmare can do many things in his dream—run, hide, fight, scream, jump off a cliff, etc.—but no change from any one of these behaviors to another would ever terminate the nightmare. We shall henceforth refer to this kind of change as first-order change. The one way out of a dream involves a

change from dreaming to waking. Waking, obviously, is no longer a part of the dream, but a change to an altogether different state. This kind of change will from now on be referred to as second-order change. (Watzlawick et al., 1974, p. 10)

Applying these ideas to the family, Level I change is change in the fairly specific patterns of behavior and transformation processes (Burr, 1991). An example of first-order change is to change a family rule or norm. Another example is to change who does what in the family chores. A third example is to change the way a family ritual, such as a birthday, is celebrated as a child matures. These changes are changes within fairly specific processes in a family system, and they do not change the fundamental aspects or the basic structural parts of the system.

Level II change is that in processes that are at a higher level of abstraction in the system. The system changes so that it is fundamentally different. This is similar to Watzlawick's example of waking up from a dream and changing the system that contained the actions in the dream.

An example in family systems is to change metarules such as the rules about how rules are made and changed. A second example is to reframe the role of chores in a family. Assume, for example, that a family had a business-like or economic orientation toward chores and believed that getting the chores done efficiently is most important. If the family were to reframe the nature of chores so they were viewed as a means for promoting closeness, sharing, interaction, and caring for family members, then this would be a second-order change.

A third example would be to make a major change in the way all of the rituals in a family are celebrated. Some research suggests that when alcohol has a central place in family rituals it tends to increase the likelihood that alcoholism will be passed from one generation to the next (Steinglass, Bennett, Wolin, & Reiss, 1987, chap. 10). If a family that learns about this research were to change the way that alcohol is viewed and no longer use it as a part of its rituals, then this would be a Level II change.

Reiss's (1981) concept of family paradigms deals with a third level of abstraction. Family paradigms refer to a family's basic assumptions about life. Examples of paradigmatic beliefs include whether or not humans are good, whether life is fair, and so on. These beliefs or basic assumptions of life provide the basis for family goals and values. These beliefs guide thought and action in families and provide the basis for meaning and purpose. Reiss contended that change in these basic beliefs happens very seldom and that change at this abstract level of family systems usually involves severe stress.

Reiss (1981) did not integrate his concept with Watzlawick's ideas about Level I and II change. However, Burr (1991) has suggested that it is helpful to integrate these ideas and think about all three levels of abstraction in family systems. He suggested that we use an integrated conceptual scheme where the term *Level I* is used to refer to the stability and change in the fairly specific processes in family systems such as rules and transformation processes. The term *Level II* is used to refer to stability and change in processes that are at an intermediate level of abstraction. These would include what Watzlawick et al. (1974) termed *second-order change* and what Constantine (1986) called the *family regime*. The term *Level III* is used to refer to the highly abstract processes such as family paradigms and values.

A New Theoretical Idea: Levels of Stress

Thinking about three levels of abstraction leads to an exciting new theoretical idea: Family coping processes have three different levels of abstraction, and families probably move through them in a developmental way. Figure 3.2 is an attempt to diagram this idea.

We are proposing that when families encounter stressful situations they first try to change their Level I processes. For example, they may change family rules, rearrange responsibilities, or change who does what. They change the way they are disciplining or the way they are spending money.

If changes in Level I processes are successful, then the family moves into a period of recovery and has no need to try coping processes that create Level II or III changes. However, if the Level I processes are not successful, then families try to create changes in the more fundamental Level II processes.

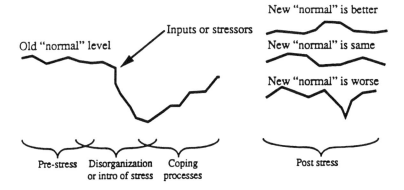

Figure 3.2 Levels of Stress in Family Systems

It is likely that many coping strategies may be used to make changes at any level, and a family may try to change at any level for a long period of time before moving to a different level. Also, it may be that all families do not go through this developmental sequence all of the time. There may be certain stressor events, types of families, and situations in which families may skip a level or vary in other ways. To better clarify what is involved in the proposed developmental sequence, the following paragraphs explain in more detail what we think is involved in each level.

Level I Stress

When families experience Level I stress, the coping strategies they use are attempts to change relatively specific patterns in the behavior of family members or to make changes in the role expectations or rules in the family system (Sluzki, 1983; Watzlawick et al., 1974). We suspect that when families first encounter stress, they tend to use a wide range of coping strategies that create Level I change. At this level of stress, families try to hammer out new rules and new transformation processes, sometimes consciously and sometimes unconsciously, but the basic metalevel of the system remains intact. *Metalevel* refers to rules about the rules, rules about changing rules, rules about the negotiating of rules, and so on.

The arrival of a first child is a Level I stress for many families. It is stressful because the family is not able to attain its goals with its

customary transformation processes, and new rules and new processes need to be devised. Usually, however, most couples are able
to work through this stress without changing the basic structure of
family processes. They still make rules, make decisions, and relate
to each other in the same basic ways after the family settles down
with the new child.

This example is especially helpful in understanding the differences between Level I and II change; when most people begin to
think with a systems perspective, they assume that a change in the
system's membership by the addition of a new person is a change
in a fundamental aspect of the system: its membership. Also, it
usually involves a change in the system's specific rules and transformation processes. However, our experience suggests that it is
usually not much of a change in the structure of the basic or fundamental processes in the system. The husband and wife usually
maintain the same basic Level II processes such as (a) their method
of governing their family, (b) their method of decision making, (c)
whether they are basically cooperative or competitive, and (d) how
much they express love, concern, and compassion.

Also, when a family has its first child, there is usually little
change in Level III processes. For example, there is usually little
change in such things as (a) their basic values, (b) their philosophy
of life, (c) their sacred versus secular orientation, (d) their beliefs
about having a business-like or economic orientation versus a concern with the emotional parts of life, (e) their assumptions about
being open or closed and random or synchronic (Constantine,
1986), and (f) their tendencies toward closure, configuration, and
coordination (Reiss, 1981).

Families can do many things to try coping with stressors while
staying at the lowest level of abstraction. They can get new information, seek help from neighbors or relatives, turn to community
agencies for assistance, talk to friends about how they have dealt
with similar situations, have family councils to decide how to adjust
things in the family to deal with the new situation, and so forth.

Level II Stress

When families are able to deal effectively with stressor events by
using Level I processes, we suspect they stop focusing on the

stressful situation and return to their normal level of functioning. As they resume their normal operation, the attention they were giving to the stressful situation shifts to other things such as careers, friends, arts, sports, leisure, service, school, and a variety of other interests.

However, when Level I coping strategies are not successful, families gradually find themselves in a progressively more difficult situation. This is shown in Figure 3.2 with Level II stress. In these situations, merely rearranging rules or changing the superficial or obvious aspects of the family are not enough, and the family needs to make more fundamental or metalevel changes.

Several examples of this process help illustrate what can be involved with Level II crises. If a child is misbehaving in a fairly serious way, we suspect a family will initially try to use Level I strategies to cope. They will do such things as use more severe disciplinary methods such as grounding the child, restricting privileges, withholding resources, or changing rules. In some situations, these Level I changes are adequate, but if not, then the parents may need to reevaluate their entire approach toward discipline; this would involve thinking about a Level II process. The parents may change the way in which they relate to the child. For example, they may realize that they have been using methods of discipline that are appropriate for a young child, while theirs is old enough to need more "adult" methods of discipline.

Another example occurs in some marriages when one spouse wants to change the relationship. A husband and wife may have grown up in fairly traditional families where males were dominant and females submissive, but one spouse may gradually decide that she or he does not like that type of relationship. This type of change would usually be a stressor event, and merely changing Level I rules may not be enough. For example, "letting" her have her own checking account, get a job, or take classes at the university may not be enough. The couple may need to rearrange some fundamental aspects of their relationship. They may need to change the idea that the husband is supposed to "let" the wife do things. They may need to move to an egalitarian relationship in which neither spouse is responsible for what the other does. Changes such as these are more complicated, abstract, and fundamental than Level I changes because they deal with the rules about the rules.

Level III Stress

When families are able to deal effectively with stressor events by using Level I or II processes, we suspect they tend to return to their normal level of functioning. However, in some situations, families are not able to manage the new system inputs with these strategies. When this occurs, these families gradually slip into a deeper and more serious stressful situation. This is diagrammed in Figure 3.2 as Level III stress.

When this happens, the very fabric of the family is in trouble, and the paradigmatic assumptions are called into question. The family's basic philosophy and orientations to life are examined, and these basic beliefs may evolve, change, or be discarded or reconstructed.

Many examples can illustrate these Level III changes. When families make basic changes in the ways they relate to their environment or in their beliefs about who they can count on when the chips are down, these are paradigm changes. When families change their ideas about fundamental spiritual or theological ideas or the role of the spiritual part of life, this would be a Level III change. Also, changes in beliefs about whether people are inherently good or bad and how much to be differentiated from kin are fundamental parts of family ideology.

The following example illustrates the sequential pattern we believe occurs in family systems. A family that did not believe in drug use would face a stressor event if it found that its teenage son was taking drugs. The family may first use one of many Level I coping strategies to create change. For example, the parents could talk to the son about the danger of drugs or could express their disapproval. If these particular Level I methods do not work, then the family might try other Level I changes such as making the son come home earlier, grounding him, or taking away such resources as money. There is no limit to the specific Level I changes that families can try.

If the Level I methods take care of the stress, then additional coping strategies do not need to be tried. However, it they do not work, then the family would eventually resort to more fundamental Level II changes. They may try to change their basic parenting methods, get professional assistance to make other changes, change where the child lives, or otherwise change the basic family structure.

If these Level II methods do not work, then the family may eventually question some of its basic beliefs. For example, it may adopt a more fatalistic view of life and conclude that things will happen as they will and the family has less control over its world than it thought. The family may rearrange its priorities in life and become more or less involved in trying to change community values and structure. For example, it may reevaluate its beliefs about the appropriateness of drugs or laws. It may decide to oppose the legal system or crusade for more stringent laws. It may decide to become more daring and join the child in exploring the use of drugs. These changes in beliefs may not just concern drugs, they may expand to influence other parts of life such as how the family relates to relatives, friends, or the larger community.

SUMMARY

This chapter argues that the ABC-X part of family stress theories is fundamentally positivistic, and therefore many assumptions are incompatible with the nonpositivistic systemic ideas that have been developed in the last several decades. We suggest that the time has come to separate the more deterministic ABC-X model from the less indeterministic systems ideas and have two different theories. We believe this separation will make the systems theory more useful in developing new theoretical insights, in doing empirical research, and in making the theory more relevant for practitioners. This chapter is an attempt to examine the systems theory of family stress and identify several new theoretical and empirical questions. These questions are then partially tested in the later chapters of this volume. We hope the outcome is expansion of the theory of family stress by the development of new theoretical ideas.

NOTE

1. One body of literature that is not included in this analysis is Lazarus's models of stress. His work is not included because his approach is an individualistic and psychic approach that deals with individual stress. He did not attempt to develop a model of family stress. There are, of course, similarities: He pays attention to subjective appraisal, meaning, and coping strategies. But the level of analysis is so different from the issues in this chapter that if we were to try to include his model, then we would be introducing some of the same kinds of inconsistencies we are trying to correct.

FOUR

Research Design

We began this project with several preconceptions about what we wanted: solid data but also the flexibility to look at more than numbers. We also wanted data that would help us learn more about some of the subtle and intricate processes in family systems and deal with the ideas behind the numbers. To accomplish these goals, we decided early in the project to combine quantitative and qualitative data.

Qualitative and quantitative data each have unique advantages and disadvantages in studying family stress. Among the advantages of quantitative data are that they allow coding and quantifying of information for analysis with inferential statistics, definitive testing of hypotheses, and comparison of our findings with other studies. Because our project had several explicit hypotheses and objectives, we developed different ways to quantify various parts of the data.

The search for qualitative data provided several different contributions to this project: It helped us look for unanticipated patterns in families' responses. Examples of theorized relationships and findings about specific family situations give data more meaning. Qualitative data also provided unique insights into the subtleties and complexities of family stress that have not been adequately studied when quantitative methods alone are used (Walker, 1985). We also found that our qualitative analyses of the data helped us understand some of the reasons certain quantitative findings occurred as they did. Also, variations in the qualitative data helped provide additional information about some of the research questions and issues addressed in the project.

The combination of qualitative and quantitative methods also helped us deal with several methodological difficulties in the family stress literature. One of these is that the combination of methods best deals with the complexity in the family realm. Walker (1985) argued for the need to use a contextual approach when studying family stress. Our research supported the notion that "the complexity of the stress process cannot be handled with predictable responses, universal stages, or identical points of resolution" (p. 832). Thus our research was an attempt to contextualize family stress by trying to take into account individuals, the husband-wife dyad, the familial setting, and, to some extent, the social, community, and cultural networks in the data-collection process.

In summary, we tried to integrate quantitative and qualitative research methods in a complementary manner. This integration strengthened the project in ways that would not have been possible if we had only qualitative or quantitative data.

DATA SOURCES

One of the many trade-offs in research is whether to use a large or small sample. When the resources that are available for a project are limited and modest, the compromise is between getting progressively more superficial data as the sample gets larger and progressively more depth as the sample gets smaller. After some discussion, we decided to emphasize depth rather than breadth. We thus decided to study a relatively small sample of subjects and to use a combination of interview, observation, and questionnaire methods to gather data. We also decided to spend enough time with the families that we would be able to pay attention to their perceptions and feelings, get to know them and their situations fairly well, and thereby get considerable depth.

Our study is therefore similar to studies by Koos (1946), Hill (1949), and Kantor and Lehr (1975) by having a fairly small and homogeneous sample. This approach has both limitations and advantages. We know, for example, that our findings are not related to ethnic, racial, urban, or a variety of other demographic factors. The homogeneity of our sample makes it more defensible to argue that the diversity and variation we found results from the stress rather than other variables, even without elaborate controls for variations in other factors. Even in our sample we found considerably more variance than previous research has shown.

This study sets the stage for similar research with other homogeneous but different communities. Further studies with other groups could help us gain confidence in the generalizability of these findings. Several studies with small groups give the advantages of both breadth and depth. We hope that others will be encouraged about the benefits of studying small groups and use similar methods to continue researching family stress from a systems perspective.

Another issue in family research was identified by McCubbin et al. (1980) and Boss (1987): the need to shift from studying dysfunctional families to studying many different kinds of family situations. Families who are able to endure hardships over the life span have been underrepresented in research studies, and there is a need to study strong families because stress is universally prevalent although not necessarily problematic in many families. In other words, the stressful situation may result in new levels of family functioning that are not necessarily destructive. To identify families that were able to endure stress, our sampling techniques concentrated on families who had sought help in a variety of ways or who had remained intact and maintained their residence despite the stress. That they had sought help in courts, hospitals, or other agencies is also evidence that the families had identified their own stressful situation and taken steps to alleviate it.

We conducted in-depth interviews and observations with families who had experienced one of six different types of family stressors:

1. bankruptcy,
2. a child who was sufficiently handicapped to require institutionalization,
3. a teenage child who was difficult enough to manage that professional psychiatric help was sought,
4. a child with muscular dystrophy,
5. infertility, and

6. displacement as a homemaker.

Because the circumstances of these families are each different, we used different sampling techniques to locate the different types of subjects. Our goal was to try to identify eight or nine families who had experienced each of the different stressor events and thus study some 50 families.

Sampling Bankruptcy Cases

We had two objectives in sampling families who had experienced bankruptcy. First, we believed that it would be useful to study families who had experienced the stress of bankruptcy over a period of time that was long enough to respond to questions about how they managed. Second, we needed to find families who were accessible to the research team.

To find these families, we obtained a list of all bankruptcies filed in 1989 by people served by the U.S. Bankruptcy Court that included Utah County in Utah. The list was of approximately 750 names; it was divided among members of the research team, and a random selection of respondents was made by calling every fifth name on the list. Approximately 120 names were selected. Half the names selected could not be contacted because of a disconnected phone number. Twenty percent of the remaining half refused to participate. Several families who consented to interviews could not arrange time for the interview. Thus the sample we were eventually able to study included families who had experienced bankruptcy but who also were sufficiently stable residentially that they could be located in the same geographic area approximately a year later and who were also willing to participate in a research study. We eventually included seven families who had experienced this particular stressor.

Institutionally Handicapped Children

Families with institutionally handicapped children were accessed through a private care center. This center is "home" for 50 to 75 children with multiple handicaps. After obtaining permission from the owner of the care center, initial contact with families of these children was made by the head teacher. At the discretion of the teacher, couples were contacted who (a) had children who were full-time residents rather than outpatients, (b) were willing to talk about the stress they had endured as a family, and (c) were likely to participate.

Of the families contacted, 11 agreed to participate in the study. Some lived in neighboring states, and interviews were arranged if possible. Of these 11 families, 9 were interviewed about the stress they experience as a result of a child who is so severely handicapped that private care is required.

Troubled Teens

The troubled teen population to which we had access were families who had adolescent children with behavioral problems distressing enough to be admitted to the adolescent treatment center of the local regional medical center. To gain access to this population we obtained permission from the unit director of the center, the psychiatrist in charge of mental health services at the hospital, and a hospital review committee. After obtaining permission, we obtained a random sample from the program book of 20 names of adolescents who had been admitted to the center between January 1989 and June 1990.

The program book lists patients in order of date of admission, and names were taken on a rotation basis that ensured sampling of the entire time period. A member of the research team then called parents of the adolescents to explain our research project and ask for their participation. Of the original 20 names, the majority had disconnected or incorrect phone numbers, so an additional sample was drawn. From this random list, 13 families were located, and 11 responded positively to the phone request for their participation in the study. Despite several attempts, 2 of the 11 were never reached to obtain written consent. Two others who consented in writing could not arrange an acceptable interview time and were not interviewed. One family was reluctant to participate and asked for a consent form but never returned the form with written permission. The sampling process resulted in a total of four interviews with families who had experienced the stress of a troubled teen. We had initially hoped to have several more families with this particular challenge, but we eventually settled for what we were able to acquire.

Chronically Ill Children

We wanted to include a group of families who had coped with a chronic medical condition. We considered several possibilities, such as cystic fibrosis, muscular dystrophy, automobile accidents, and mental retardation. We contacted the state Muscular Dystrophy Association office and were able to get help with the project.

We decided to include families who had a dystrophic child who was 12 or older or families who had children who had died within the preceding one or two years. This limitation on the population sample was an effort to identify families who had experienced later stages of the illness and the stress that accompanies the ongoing, degenerative nature of the Duchenne type of muscular dystrophy. This type of muscular dystrophy usually is genetically transmitted and is found only in boys.

The local Muscular Dystrophy Association agreed to solicit families to participate in the study. Given the parameters of the desired population, the patient services coordinator started at the top of the patient list and called for contact permission. Two families declined participation, mostly because they did not want to talk about the child who had died. Twelve families agreed to participate. One of the 12 families eventually declined to be interviewed, so 11 families from three counties were interviewed.

Infertility

RESOLVE is a local and national organization that offers information and support to couples experiencing infertility. Most states have chapters that meet periodically, publish local newsletters, and offer assistance to couples seeking additional support and information about infertility. Although many more couples are experiencing infertility than are RESOLVE members, the research team reasoned that the organization's members would be appropriate for purposes of this study because the membership provides a readily identifiable segment of the infertile couple population. RESOLVE members usually have been medically diagnosed as infertile or as having significant fertility difficulties. Members' stress levels have reached the stage where support or information is actively sought. RESOLVE members are further along in the process of dealing with infertility and thus have experienced the process of coping with a significant stressor.

Officers of the local RESOLVE chapter were contacted about the availability of couples for this study. Officers agreed to contact group members to solicit participation in the study. To maintain members' confidentiality, chapter officers agreed to affix address labels to envelopes containing letters that invited members of RESOLVE to participate in the study. Following the initial contact, each couple was contacted by a member of the research team by telephone, and an appointment was made for the researcher to conduct the interview in the person's home. Of the 40 letters mailed to RESOLVE members, approximately 30% (12 respondents) expressed interest in participation. Of the 12 couples, 1 was out of the area and 1 could not schedule a time for the interview. A total of 10 couples were interviewed who had experienced the stress of infertility.

Displaced Homemaker

The population of women who had been displaced from their role as homemaker was accessed through a community program designed to help women manage the consequences of their displacement. Through the program office, brief letters were handed out to participants to see if they would be willing to be interviewed by our group. The letter detailed who was conducting the research, the purpose of the project, and what would be required of the interviewees. The letter page provided room for volunteers to give personal information if they wished to be contacted. This information was then returned to the office for pickup by a member of the research team. After receiving responses from 14 volunteers, interviewers randomly selected 10 to contact for interviews. Nine interviews with displaced homemakers were completed.

DATA COLLECTION

Data were collected in the respondents' homes. We believed that we would get more depth, more accuracy, and less guarded information if we were on each family's turf rather than in a more impersonal setting such as a laboratory or office.

The sessions with the families lasted several hours. We used different methods to gather information. We had the families complete questionnaires, and we observed the behaviors of individuals and the interaction patterns between individuals during the interview. We also interviewed them with some time devoted to open-ended interviewing and some time allocated to more structured interview questions with additional probes.

Most of the time the data gathering was all conducted in one session. In some situations, however, we returned to some of the homes to get additional information. We audiotaped the conversations and later transcribed the tapes to facilitate the data analysis.

Several complicated issues needed to be considered in designing the data-gathering methods. One issue was identified by McCubbin et al. (1980) and Reiss (1981): In daily life, stressors are not kept separate from dependent variables, family responses, and adjustments, so it is not always clear whether family stress is part of the response or an inherent part of the stressor. To avoid confounding the stressors with the stress and responses, we relied on the perceptions of the families and tried to maintain a conversational relationship in which we and the families could clarify what we were saying and ask questions when we were unsure of what was being said.

Another prominent issue was systematic bias brought on by the order in which various topics were discussed: The order itself might influence what was said. To minimize such systematic bias, we randomized the order of the questions asked during the interviews so that response patterns would be unrelated to question patterns in the information sought.

Another issue is that the many aspects of stress, such as amount of time a family is involved in stress or who is involved, are perceived differently by different families and members of families. To help deal with these differences, we asked family members to specify the time periods they believed were important and who was involved. Thus the perceptions of time were unique to each respondent and depended on his or her particular situation, whether experiencing something relatively short-term such as bankruptcy or long-term such as a child with muscular dystrophy.

We developed a rather elaborate schedule to guide the interviewers. The schedule consisted of questions designed to elicit conversational responses, several questionnaires to which family members responded, and rating scales for the interviewer to complete.

Interview Schedule

The interview schedule was designed to investigate multiple aspects of stress. Specific strategies to inquire about a particular aspect of stress were designed and then incorporated in a comprehensive interview schedule. This comprehensive interview schedule was planned to accomplish two ends: (a) avoiding the bias of having one team collect all the data from families experiencing one particular type of stressor and (b) achieving uniform data collection by multiple researchers who were interviewing families in different circumstances while also allowing for the families' individual differences.

The interview guide began with a section to introduce the study and collect demographic information. Each respondent was then asked to rank the overall difficulty of his or her stressful situation by making a comparison to the Holmes and Rahe chart. This was an effort to assess the relative severity of the multiple kinds of stressors.

Next, individual respondents charted their individual perceptions of how the family functioned both overall and in nine other areas of family life:

1. togetherness and cohesion,
2. marital satisfaction,
3. communication,
4. daily routines,
5. contention,
6. family development,
7. leadership,
8. family rituals, and
9. emotional climate.

The nine areas were not represented in any particular order; instead, charts were randomized for each family at the time of the interview. Each respondent filled in a time line according to his or her perception of the stressful situation before graphing individual responses to the stressful situation. On a scale of +4 to −4, respondents indicated a range from "substantially better" to "paralyzed." A final chart provided space for respondents to chart the amount of attention (time, effort, or energy) needed for the stressful situation at different times. Answers ranged from "all-consuming" to "moderate" to "minimal" over a period of time specified by each respondent.

The next part of the interview guide was a questionnaire for recording perceptions of how couples managed the stressful situation individually. The husband and wife filled out the questionnaire separately and discussed their answers with each other and the interviewer. The questionnaire included Likert-type scales for assessing the effects of 80 specific strategies and the amount of time, effort, or energy spent on each strategy and how helpful it was.

A modified Q-sort was used to gather information about the stages at which families used specific strategies. Husbands and wives worked together on the Q-sort. They used 3×5 cards that described the 80 specific strategies and sorted each strategy into piles to show the different times they thought they had used the strategy during their stressful period. Stages included immediately after the stress began, not immediately but fairly soon after, quite a bit later, much later, and not at all.

The interview ended with a discussion. Couples were encouraged to compare their answers, talk about their similarities and differences, and make any other comments they would like. We asked each family what it had done that had helped the most and what it would recommend to other families encountering the same type of situation.

Following the interview, the researcher made observations about the family system and ranked the family on several scales. Areas of interest included the following:

- quality of communication;
- power, assertiveness, and dominance in the family;
- chronic anxiety (resentment, animosity, tension) in the family emotional climate;
- family paradigms (economic versus emotional, sacred versus secular);
- quality of respect for others in the family system;
- level of compassion and caring in the family (low to great);
- definition of the stressful situation (not serious to extremely serious); and
- ability of the family to manage the situation (poor, moderately good, excellent).

Training and Pilot Interviews

Our research team consisted of two faculty supervisors, four undergraduate students, and four graduate students. We met weekly during the project's design stage. The students participated in the literature review, research problem selection, and instrument design. In designing the data-gathering instruments, the group went over each part many times in detail to help the interviewers know how to deal with potential questions.

The interviewers first practiced by interviewing one another. Then two pilot interviews were conducted to train members of the research team and to test the instrument. One interview was with a family who had a child with muscular dystrophy, and the other was with a family who had dealt with the challenges of infertility.

The entire research team attended these two interviews. One individual did the interviewing, the others observed. This made these sessions a little more public than later interviews, but we believed it would help all interviewers function in a similar manner.

As a result of the pilot interviews, minor clarifications were made in the instructions, and two changes were made in the data collection. We decided to eliminate the category of "all through" the stressful situation in the Q-sort because we found that couples tended to generalize too quickly without taking the time to decide when they began to use a particular strategy. Thus by our elimination of the "all through" category, respondents had to be more specific.

We also decided to randomize the charts that respondents would complete about the nine areas of family functioning. By randomizing the charts at the time of each interview, we hoped to eliminate any bias in the data that might result simply because the information had been collected in the same order each time.

Collecting the Data

Interviews in 50 households were conducted over a 3-month period in spring 1991. Interviews included 10 couples who had experienced infertility, 11 families with muscular dystrophic children, 7 families who had experienced bankruptcy, 9 families with institutionalized children, 9 displaced homemakers, and 4 families with troubled teens. Data were coded to ensure confidentiality.

We were unable to get all of the information from all 50 families about all of the parts of the questionnaires and interviews: Some families became tired of the process or had interfering complications. We were able to gather all of the data for 46 families and most of the data we wanted on the other four. These differences, however, mean slightly different totals (Ns) in some samples in later chapters reporting findings.

Our respondents were 32 adult males and 46 adult females. The average number of children was three. Ten households reported no children currently living at home. Sixty-three percent of the households reported themselves as first marriages, 13% as remarriages, and 24% with single heads of household. Number of years married ranged from less than 1 to 41. Ages of participants ranged from 21 to 65, with an average age of 39 for men and 36 for women. Eighty percent of the households listed Latter-day Saints (Mormon) as their religious preference, 17% listed "other," and less than 3% listed "none."

One limitation of the methodology of this project is that children were not included in the population sampling. Boss (1987) claimed that family stress management involves both group and individual management of stress. It follows that the family as a group is not managing successfully if even one member manifests distress symptoms. Children certainly are important family members, but we decided to sacrifice the depth that might be gained by including children in the sample for a broader cross-section of families in general. A useful addition to the literature would be an analysis of children's responses to family stress.

DATA ANALYSIS

The research team was divided into four groups for the analysis process. The results of their analyses are presented in the four findings chapters. Chapter 5 reports what we learned about the overall functioning of families. Chapter 6 discusses the way in which nine specific aspects of families change over time. Chapter 8 tells which coping strategies were used the most and how helpful and harmful the strategies were. Chapter 9 considers the issue of whether families use Level I, II, and III coping strategies in a specific time sequence.

Each chapter had some unique method of analysis. These more chapter-specific and detailed aspects of the data analysis are discussed in each chapter.

During the analysis phase of the project, the research team met regularly to discuss what each group was doing and finding. The various groups also read drafts of the manuscripts to try to be as thorough as possible and guard against bias and error in the analysis and interpretation of the data. The writing was continuously reviewed by members of the team to protect against premature closure and conclusions not supported by data.

After each research team had analyzed the data for its chapter and reached its conclusions, we divided the audio tapes among team members and reexamined them all. We had three goals in reanalyzing the tapes:

1. to discover insights or conclusions that had not previously appeared in the data analysis,
2. to find corroborating or disputing evidence for the observations or conclusions we had reached, and
3. to find additional comments by the families that would illustrate important insights and conclusions.

SUMMARY

The design in this project was to gather in-depth data about what families experienced as they coped with one of six different stressful situations: bankruptcy, infertility, a difficult teenager, muscular dystrophy, displaced homemaker, or a child who was sufficiently handicapped to need institutionalization. We used a combination of qualitative and quantitative methods in gathering and analyzing the data. The findings are reported in Chapters 5, 6, 8, and 9.

F I V E

Changes in Overall Family Functioning

Chapter 3 described the roller-coaster pattern of family response to stress. Several new theoretical questions also were raised in that chapter. The new questions arose because the nonpositivistic paradigmatic approach and systemic theory lead us in different directions than earlier research had gone.

In earlier research we assumed that the roller-coaster pattern is universal of families encountering stress. However, when we think about stress as a process, it sensitizes us to the reality that families experience this process in diverse ways. This led us to question the idea that all families experience the roller-coaster pattern. The purpose of this chapter is to examine our data to determine how universal the roller-coaster pattern is.

Several events in the early stages of the current research influenced the way we approached this question. We observed that the contemporary family science literature universally assumes that the roller-coaster model is "the" way in which family systems respond to stressors. It is the model used in family science textbooks, reviews of the literature, and research papers and monographs (Hill, 1971; Olson, Sprenkle, & Russell, 1979; Reiss & Oliveri, 1991). It is such an intuitive and apparently commonsense model that it has become the standard description of family functioning under stress and the basic assumption on which theory, education, and therapy are built.

As we began to formulate the research questions for this project, we found ourselves questioning the universality of the roller-coaster model. We observed that several scholars have suggested considerable variation in the way families respond to any kind of input (Constantine, 1986), and some have suggested this to be especially so with stress-producing inputs (Reiss, 1981; Walker, 1985). Also, during one discussion, several members of our research team shared the way their families had responded to several stressful situations, and we were struck by how different some of them were from the roller-coaster pattern.

For example, the 1989 death of the mother of one member of our team brought his father, brother, two sisters, and himself together in a way they had never known before. "Jealousies and differences of opinion disappeared as we pulled together to bolster Dad and to make arrangements for the funeral. We communicated better; we completed household tasks better; we made decisions better; we felt closer to our spouses. It's true our emotions went down. We were shocked, saddened, hurt, angry, guilt-ridden. We went through the stages of coping with death. But our family functioning (which the roller-coaster model is supposed to explain) clearly improved under that particular stressor. It returned to normal after the crisis passed."

Another member of our research team went through a similar episode when her brother died suddenly. Her family also did not experience the decrease in functioning that is predicted by the roller-coaster pattern.

Another member of our team had a son who died of muscular dystrophy in 1984 at age 23. The parents experienced many years of challenges as their son lived for a dozen years in a wheelchair. They experienced many crises, strains, and ups and downs, but it was not until the last year of his life that the family functioning experienced a decline. Family members believed that they were enriched in many ways and had learned patience, service, and love in ways they may not have learned without their challenges.

These theoretical ideas and personal experiences led us to doubt the universal application of Koos's model. We therefore formed a working hypothesis that the roller-coaster model describes some, but not all, family experiences. We then became interested in trying to see if we could discover any other patterns in the way family systems respond to stress.

After we developed our hypothesis, we noted that Hill (1949) had developed two diagrams of the ways families respond to stress that were quite different from the roller coaster. One was a straight line, representing families that adjusted quickly and well to separation. The other was an upward line that indicated an improvement in functioning, no crisis, and no recovery. Hill characterized these upward patterns as "poor adjustment to separation" (Hill, 1949, p. 99). Families in this group had poor relationships to begin with and were much better off with the husband and father gone. It is interesting to us that these other patterns—the straight line and the upward line—appear to have been viewed as anomalies rather than as normal patterns. One reasons for this, we suspect, was that the guiding paradigm led researchers to focus on issues of causality such as whether the A, B, and C factors caused stress. Not until we consciously separated the two paradigmatic approaches did the issue of diversity become salient rather than remain an anomaly.

METHODOLOGY

To test our speculations, we created a set of charts that would allow families to draw graphs representing their personal struggles with stress. Knowing they had never heard of Koos, we wanted to see if they would draw something similar to the roller-coaster model. Because family experiences varied greatly and over widely different time periods, we devised a grid with 12 cells along the x-axis and 8 cells along the y-axis. This grid is illustrated in Figure 5.1.

We allowed the respondents to establish their own time lines on the x-axis. Each cell could represent a month, two months, a year, or whatever was appropriate for the respondents' particular experience. Whether a family's stressor lasted 1, 5, or 20 years, their graph fit within the same-sized grid. On the y-axis, we established a normal line, which meant "normal for us." In other words, we asked families to think of what was normal in their household and

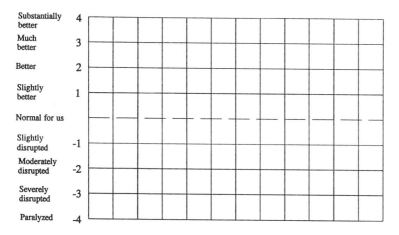

Figure 5.1 Overall Family Functioning Grid

not to compare themselves with other families. Above the normal line, we allowed for functioning to get slightly better, better, much better, and substantially better. Below the line, the possibilities were slightly disrupted, moderately disrupted, severely disrupted, and paralyzed. We suggested that family functioning could go either way under stress, and we then let the families plot their situations as they saw them.

We took time explaining what we meant by family functioning in an effort to get a uniform concept. We also asked the families to fill out charts on nine specific areas of family functioning (discussed in the next chapter) before having them fill out the chart on overall family functioning. We thought this would help them be able to back off and make an overall assessment. We also asked respondents to label critical events during their stressful experiences by noting them on the bottom of the grid.

Our objectives in using this self-report method were to see whether the patterns that emerged from our respondents' heads were similar to the roller-coaster model and to see if we could discover new patterns. Our study was similar to the Koos research in dealing with a small number of families (51 families and 82 individuals), and it was restricted to a small geographic region. Also, only the adults in the families participated in our interviews. Because our emphasis was on more general patterns in family processes and less on searching for determinants, variance, or causes of family behaviors, we decided to forego a large sample and concentrate on discussing the issues in-depth with the families. Given the size and nature of our sample, the variance we found seems even more significant. Our findings are suggestive, and replications are needed before we can be confident that our findings can be generalized.

Our method of analysis was to examine the charts visually to see patterns in the ways the families responded to the stressors. We also listened to the tapes to try to better understand what the families were telling us.

Two members of the research team, Brent Harker and Shawna Parrish, did the initial inspection of the charts, sorting them several times until results of the sort were the same each time. What emerged were five clearly distinguishable models. After our initial analysis, we discussed the results with the other members of the research team to see if the results were meaningful to them. Then several other members of the research group sorted them separately, and their results varied by no more than 3 out of 82 charts. After identifying the models, we conducted Chi-square and analysis-of-variance tests, looking for information about which variables might interact with others. We will first present the patterns that emerged and then the tests.

FINDINGS ON FAMILY FUNCTIONING

Roller-Coaster Pattern

Our first observation was that a sizable number of families experienced the roller-coaster pattern. Of the 82 individuals who filled out family functioning charts, 42 (51.2%) described a clear decline in the quality of the family functioning followed by a recovery. Some of their graphs were so strikingly similar to the roller-coaster model that they appeared to have been copied from a textbook. Others were quite different but still included the essential decline and recovery. Figure 5.2 shows the graphs from two of the families who experienced the roller-coaster pattern.

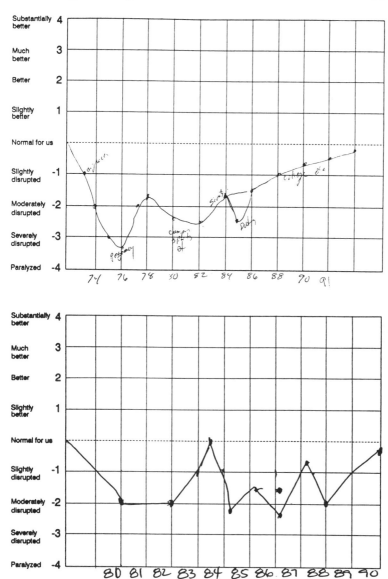

Figure 5.2 Two Examples of the Roller-Coaster Model

One woman we interviewed expressed eloquently how it feels
to experience a deep decline in family functioning and then gradually

recover. She and her husband were forced to institutionalize their daughter after the infant suffered severe neurological damage at four months of age.

"Oh, it was so devastating. I remember when it first happened, I told [my husband], I said, 'I wish she would just have died,' because I had been through so many severe deaths in my life, and I knew how to handle that, but it was terrible. . . .

"When we went to pick her up [at the institution for a visit] she had lost so much weight, and she was tiny anyways, and he [my husband] was very angry at me, and he stayed very angry and threw it up to me that it was my decision and that I was doing this to her for nearly a year. And then, finally, we started seeing . . . that . . . that it was—even though it wasn't the best situation—it was something that really needed to be done. I'd been to the doctor, and he said, 'You can't do this. You can either plan to get better or you can plan your funeral. You can't continue to do this.' The stress was so high. . . .

"It was very hard for him [my husband] to come home and have his family blown apart. He was used to leaving in the morning and having us all together and coming home and we were all together. It was very, very hard on him, and he didn't want her to go away. And as the years went by, it got better, and we both could see, he started to see and accept it. Neither one of us have liked it or feel like it's the best thing, but it's the best thing for our situation."

Increased Model

The second pattern we detected in the data involved 15 respondents, 18.3% of the group. They experienced a clear increase in the quality of their family functioning while under stress. They drew some ups and downs, but there was no initial sharp decline, and the slope of their lines was clearly upward. We grouped their charts under what we called the *increased model*. The charts in Figure 5.3 illustrate the kind of response patterns we included in this model.

The following comments from one family illustrate this pattern. The parents demonstrate a reserve of strength that helped them see

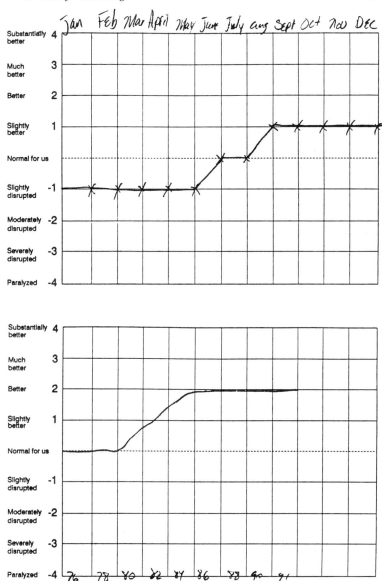

Figure 5.3 Two Examples of the Increased Model

their son's muscular dystrophy as almost normal and to improve
continually their family functioning. Their son died as a teenager,

and the wife suffered a paralyzing affliction even as they dealt
with the muscular dystrophy.

WIFE: It was a stress, but it wasn't overwhelming. The illness was,
          you know, hard to deal with, but it wasn't overwhelming.
          It was like everyday-type living. Each year he would lose
          more and more function. In the last years, he couldn't feed
          himself, clothe himself, take care of any of his needs.

HUSBAND: But did you feel it more deeply at those times when we
          could see him losing more function, or did it pretty much—
          I'm trying to sort my thoughts out—did we or did I feel,
          you know, that it's just one more thing that we have to ad-
          just to?

WIFE: I think when he'd lose something specific, like when he
          couldn't feed himself. . . .

HUSBAND: That was traumatic.

WIFE: Traumatic. But usually it was just like, "OK, we'll do this
          and . . ." sort of just gradually take over the needs, what his
          needs were. I might be upset for a couple of hours, like,
          "Oh, that's too bad. He can't do that anymore," and I'd be
          upset, but you soon forget it and you're on with what-
          ever. . . .

HUSBAND: I think with [my wife] being with me, and us being together
          on this, it was not an insurmountable deal. I just sort of fell
          into it, you might say, taking more and more care of John.
          Carrying him into the bath and getting up at night and
          turning him, things like that. Really no big deal as far as I
          could see; you just do what you have to do. I felt I was sort
          of privileged to be able to do this for John.

No Change Model

The third pattern we detected was clearly separate from the roller-
coaster and increased models. Twelve respondents (14.6%) described
their families' functioning as remaining essentially unchanged
throughout their ordeals. Their lines were virtually flat, varying
only slightly around normal, and we called their pattern the *no
change model*. This pattern is illustrated in the charts in Figure 5.4.

These families appeared to have strengths similar to those in the
increased model. The following a brief exchange among an inter-

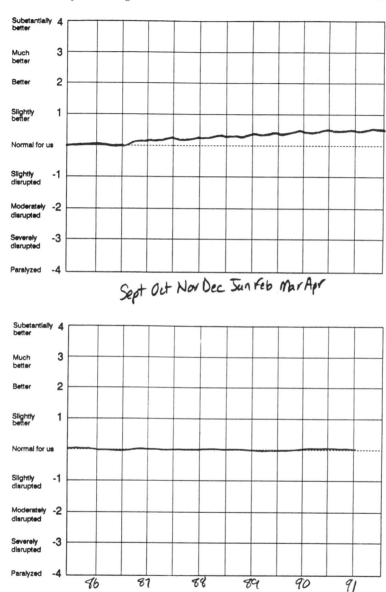

Figure 5.4 Two Examples of the No Change Model

viewer, a husband, and a wife in a family dealing with muscular dystrophy; it demonstrates how their situation remained unchanged.

INTERVIEWER: What about the way you looked at the problem?
     HUSBAND: No different than any other problem, you know.
        WIFE: It's not a problem.
     HUSBAND: Yeah, it's not a problem; at least, I don't see it as a problem.
        WIFE: I don't either; I don't see it as a problem.

Decreased Model

The fourth pattern that appeared was a decrease in family functioning that was not followed by a recovery stage. We have called
it the *decreased model*. In a sense, this is not a new discovery. Koos
observed that some families in his sample did not recover. Apparently, in their enthusiasm for the roller-coaster pattern, scholars
have ignored this pattern.

Few families experienced this pattern. Only four individuals
(4.9%) described a decline with no recovery. The two graphs in
Figure 5.5 illustrate these patterns. Only one of these families could
be said to have undergone total disintegration. She was divorced,
bankrupt, and alone. The others were in the early stages of their
stressor events, and they may yet recover. One individual described her experience as follows: "Things got really good, we
were on top of things. We bought a house, and everything just
started going down and down. The bankruptcy came, and after it
things were okay for a couple of months. Then, it just went com-
pletely down. And in November we got separated."

Mixed Model

The remainder of the families had a pattern that we eventually
called the *mixed model*. Nine individuals (11%) had families whose
functioning increased initially after they encountered their stressful situations. These respondents were different from those in the
increased model, because their increase eventually gave way to a
decline that was usually followed by a recovery.

Our research team wrestled at some length with how to view
this group because of its mixed characteristics. Its most distin-

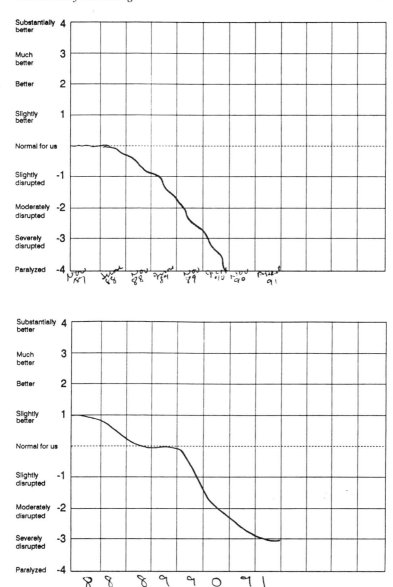

Figure 5.5 Two Examples of the Decreased Model

guishing characteristic is the initial increase in family functioning. Except for that, it resembles the roller-coaster pattern. The increase indicates a fundamentally different experience from the roller-coaster pattern developed by Koos and Hill. Therefore, we could not logically include it in the roller-coaster group. We discussed placing it in the increased group. However, the presence of the classic decline and recovery made that impossible. We decided to make a distinct category and call it the mixed model. Figure 5.6 shows two examples of these families.

Conclusions About the Five Models

Several more conclusions can be drawn from these findings. At a highly general level, our data confirm that the nature of our paradigmatic assumptions and guiding theory influence the kind of conclusions we reach. Previous theories have not sensitized us to diversity in the way families experience stress. They merely assumed that all families experience a roller-coaster pattern. Our data suggest that a systemic theory enables us to see important diversity in the way families experience stress.

More specifically, our data suggest at least five different patterns in the way family systems respond to stress. These patterns are summarized in Figure 5.7. The roller-coaster model is a good description of what happens to family functioning approximately half the time. In the other 50% of families, a sizable percent—approximately 18% in our sample—experienced an increase in functioning without any decline. Another 15% experienced no discernible change in the quality of their functioning. A small percentage, approximately 5%, experienced a decline in functioning that is permanent, and some 11% had a mixed pattern in which an increase was followed by a decrease and recovery.

Because the literature in the family field universally portrays the roller-coaster pattern as the only real way in which families respond to stress, we believe our findings to be fairly conclusive in demonstrating more variability in response patterns than is generally assumed. The roller-coaster pattern has received too much attention in the past, and the other patterns have been ignored too much.

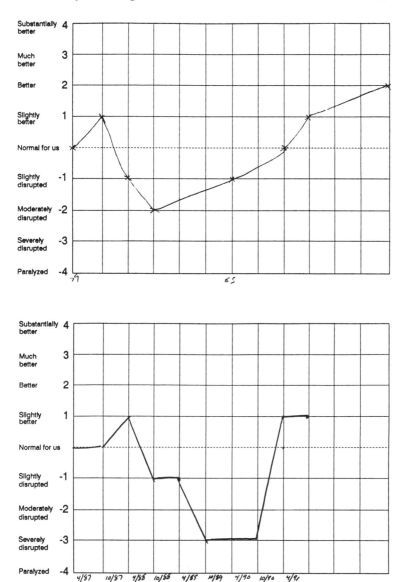

Figure 5.6 Two Examples of the Mixed Model

We repeat for emphasis that this conclusion is limited by the small number in our study and by the particular combination of

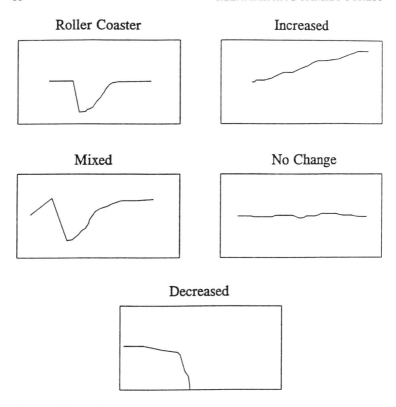

Figure 5.7 Five Models

stressors we included in the study. Our data are not very conclusive in indicating what percentage of families experiences the various patterns. All we now have are suggestive data, and we need
more replications with a wider variety of stressful situations and
different types of samples before we can be very sure what percentage of families actually experience an increase, no change, a decrease, or a mixed pattern.

One aspect of this chapter worth noting is that it changes the
nature of the questions that are being asked and the research findings that appear. The traditional approaches in the social sciences
would ask questions about how much variance is accounted for by
various independent variables. These questions would be asked
because they focus on issues of causation in a deterministic type of

scientific paradigm. This chapter is different. It has no path analyses, no regression analyses. It is not concerned about the determinants or causes of family stress. Instead, this chapter reframes the nature of family stress so that it is conceptualized as a process; we then focus on the nature of the processes.

Our goals in doing this are quite modest. All we are interested in here is whether the roller-coaster pattern is universal or whether there is diversity in the way family systems experience stress. And our data suggest much more variation than has been previously known. We wish that the resources of this project allowed us also to ask questions about which families coped effectively and ineffectively in these different patterns and what helped and hindered them. These questions would lead us closer to general principles that would help practitioners help families cope more effectively. These questions remain unasked and set the stage for future research.

The findings about diversity in this chapter have several implications for practitioners and future research. If we were to discuss these implications here, the discussion would be partial and fragmentary. Our systemic theory reminds us to be as holistic as possible. Therefore, we have opted to present all of the findings in Chapters 5 through 9 and then discuss their implications in an integrated manner. Thus the discussion of the implications of these findings for practitioners and researchers is in Chapter 10.

CORRELATES OF RESPONSE PATTERNS

After reaching the conclusion that considerable variability exists in the ways family functioning changes, we wanted to address several additional new questions.

1. Are there systematic differences in the response patterns with different kinds of stressors?
2. Are there gender differences in the perceptions of these response patterns?
3. Is the perceived seriousness of the situation related to the response patterns?

4. Are the stress-management response patterns related to the allocation of such resources as time, effort, and energy?

Stressors and Response Patterns

Both the size of our sample and the limited number of stressful situations we studied limited our ability to answer these questions, but it seemed useful to at least examine the data to spot any meaningful trends. We examined the data further by conducting a few statistical tests.

The first question we explored statistically was whether a relationship existed between specific stressors and patterns of response. The results of this tabulation are presented in Table 5.1.

Several differences are interesting. The families with displaced homemakers had the highest percentage of roller-coaster pattern, and none of these families fit the increased or mixed patterns. The greatest variability in the response pattern was with families coping with infertility. Also, the infertile families appeared less likely to experience the positive patterns and more likely to undergo negative patterns such as the roller-coaster, mixed, and decreased patterns. The two stressful situations of having a handicapped child and having a child with muscular dystrophy were relatively similar. This seems intuitively reasonable because the source of the stress in these two situations was beyond the family's control and involved the well-being of a child in the system. The stressor that showed the largest number with no change was troubled teen.

Because the N's were so small in Table 5.1, it was not meaningful to calculate inferential statistics to test the differences. However, it was possible to collapse several categories and test. Among the stressors, bankruptcy, troubled teen, and displaced homemaker fit into a category in which the perceived source of the problem could be seen as internal to the family system. Handicapped child, muscular dystrophic child, and infertility could be seen as external sources. Among the functioning patterns, decreased, roller-coaster, and mixed could be categorized as negative patterns; no change and increased could be placed in the positive category. We collapsed the groups in this manner in Table 5.2 to see if any differences were

Table 5.1 Family Functioning Patterns and Stressors

	Decreased		Roller Coaster		Mixed		No Change		Increased		Total
	No.	%	No.	%	No.	%	No.	%	No.	%	No.
Bankruptcy	1	8	7	58	0	0	0	0	4	33	12
Troubled Teen	0	0	3	50	0	0	2	33	1	17	6
Displaced Homemaker	0	0	7	78	0	0	2	22	0	0	9
Handicapped Child	0	0	7	44	2	13	3	19	4	25	16
Muscular Dystrophic Child	0	0	9	47	1	5	5	26	4	21	19
Infertility	3	15	9	45	6	30	0	0	2	10	20
Total	4	5	42	51	9	11	12	15	15	18	82

Table 5.2 Collapsed Stressors and Positive-Negative Family
          Functioning Patterns

	Negative Pattern		Positive Pattern		Total
	No.	%	No.	%	No.
Perceived Source: Internal	18	67	9	33	27
Perceived Source: External	37	67	18	33	55
Total	55	67	27	33	82

$\chi^2 = .003$
Not significant at .05 level

meaningful. The proportions were about the same, and a Chi-square test determined that the differences were not significant.

Gender Differences

As Gouldner (1988) and many others have argued, gender is a central aspect of family processes, so we wanted to look at the data to determine any meaningful gender differences. We looked at the individual graphs, tried to identify gender differences in the audio tapes, and tabulated the gender differences in several ways to see whether any gender differences were apparent. We were unable to detect any. Table 5.3 shows the tabulations when we viewed gender and whether the patterns were positive or negative; the table shows that the proportions are almost identical.

Seriousness of the Situation

The only test we conducted that showed a significant relationship between the response patterns and other variables was an analysis of variance (ANOVA) that compared family functioning patterns and respondents' definition of the seriousness of their experiences. We used the Holmes and Rahe (1967) scale to help families describe the seriousness of their situations. The scores range from 0 to 100, with 0 being not severe and 100 being equal to the

Table 5.3 Gender and Positive-Negative Family Functioning Patterns

| | Negative Pattern | | Positive Pattern | | Total |
	No.	%	No.	%	No.
Male	24	71	10	29	34
Female	37	77	11	23	48
Total	61	74	21	26	82

$$\chi^2 = .439$$
Not significant at .05 level

death of a spouse. We had the husbands and wives rank the seriousness separately and then talked with them together about their perceptions.

A slight gender difference was found in the ratings, with women rating the seriousness slightly higher. The mean was 71.3 for the women and 61.3 for the men. A *t*-test revealed this difference was significant at the .05 level, although it is not a large difference.

Table 5.4 shows the relationship between the functioning patterns and the Holmes and Rahe scores. Some of these differences are substantial. For example, the average definition of seriousness for individuals experiencing the roller-coaster pattern was 76.7; for those in the increased model, it was 49.5. These differences indicate a relationship between perception of seriousness and response patterns, and the relationship was statistically significant.

Resource Allocation and Stress

The last issue that is addressed in this chapter is whether the stress-management response patterns are related to the allocation of resources such as time, effort, and energy. We wanted to see whether patterns existed in the way families apply their resources to stress management and whether those patterns relate to patterns of family functioning.

Our first task was to find a way to measure the allocation of these resources. Failing to find any devices in the literature on family measurement, we devised our own. Our strategy was to use a

Table 5.4 ANOVA: Family Functioning Patterns and Definition of
              Seriousness

	Decreased	Roller Coaster	Mixed	No Change	Increased	Total
Mean Definition of Situation	71.0	76.7	62.8	57.3	49.5	67.0

Source of Variance	Sum of Squares	Degrees of Freedom	Estimate of Variance	F Score		
Total	36,235	80				
Between	9,220	4	2,305	6.48		
Within	27,015	76	355.46	Significant at the .05 level		

grid similar to the one for family functioning. On this grid, we used 12 cells again along the x-axis and 10 along the y-axis. The y-axis included a scale from 0 to 10, indicating minimal expenditure of time, effort, and energy at 0, moderate at 5 and all-consuming at 10. We asked the respondents to fill in their own time line along the x-axis. This time line was to match the time line on their family functioning charts. Figure 5.8 illustrates this grid.

Our expectations before we analyzed the data were based on our own reasoning and intuition, and we theorized that when families encounter stressful situations they find it necessary to allocate some of their time, energy, and effort to managing the stressful situation. Probably the more severe the stress, the greater the amount of energy required to manage it. As stress is relieved, energy expenditure goes down. When families experience a roller-coaster response pattern, our intuitive model suggests the energy expenditure will be an inverse roller-coaster with energy expenditure increasing as family functioning decreases and decreasing as family functioning increases. Thus our working hypothesis was the expectation that resource allocation would be a reciprocal image of the response pattern.

We analyzed these charts by superimposing the charts about resource allocation over the family functioning charts and trying to determine how the two lines looked together. The charts were about the same size, and the time periods they included were iden-

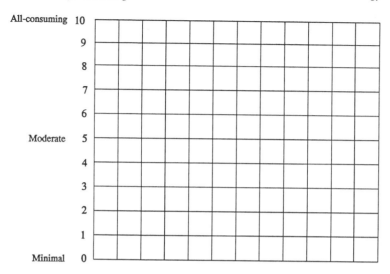

Figure 5.8 Amount of Time, Effort, and Energy Expended

tical. This led to a classification scheme and a group of models that describe both family functioning and energy expenditure.

Our findings with regard to the allocation of resources were similar to the general conclusion with the response patterns. It is too simplistic to expect all family systems to have the same pattern. We expected to find only the reciprocal pattern, but we found three fairly different patterns in the way resources were allocated. We eventually called them the *reciprocal, parallel,* and *independent patterns.*

Forty-five of our respondents (54.9%) drew the reciprocal pattern. As their family functioning decreased, energy expenditure increased and then decreased as family functioning improved. The peaks in energy expenditure matched the valleys in family functioning. It was interesting to see just how closely some of the energy charts mirrored the functioning charts even though respondents filled them out separately and did not refer to the first charts while filling out the second. Figure 5.9 shows two examples of the reciprocal pattern.

Some of the reciprocal patterns revealed slight differences in the way resources were allocated. In some cases the energy expenditure jumped immediately in response to the crisis, while in others it rose more gradually. In some cases, the peaks and valleys did not

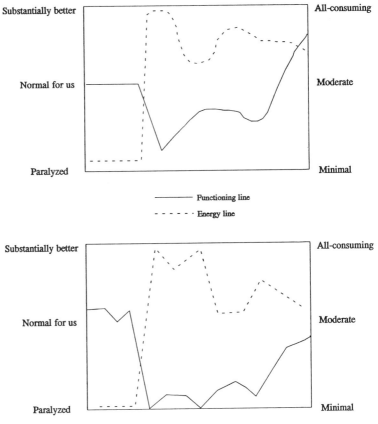

Figure 5.9 Two Examples of the Reciprocal Pattern

match exactly but indicated a delayed reaction before the families allocated their resources to the stressful situation.

The second pattern we detected was the parallel pattern, the opposite of the reciprocal pattern. Energy expenditure dipped and rose in tandem with family functioning. Twelve individuals (14.6%) reported this pattern, and Figure 5.10 shows two examples.

Parallel patterns here were not as synchronous as reciprocal patterns. The lines were roughly parallel, enough so that we could see a correlation between them, although the energy line lagged behind the functioning line.

The third pattern we detected occurred in 25 cases (30.5%). With these families, the energy line appeared to be independent of the

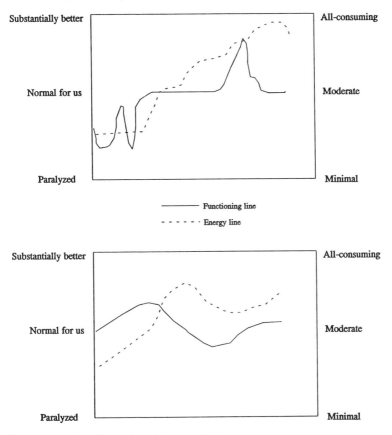

Figure 5.10 Two Examples of the Parallel Pattern

functioning line. The charts in Figure 5.11 show this pattern. In these situations, the energy expenditure varied greatly, and it did not seem to be related to the family functioning.

We were curious about whether these three ways of allocating resources were related to the roller-coaster, increased, no change, and decreased models of family functioning. We therefore created Table 5.5 to see how they were related.

What is notable about this table is that the reciprocal pattern is clearly associated with the roller-coaster model, and the independent pattern is clearly associated with the no change model. That relationship between independent and no change is almost an artifact of this construction, however. When family functioning is a

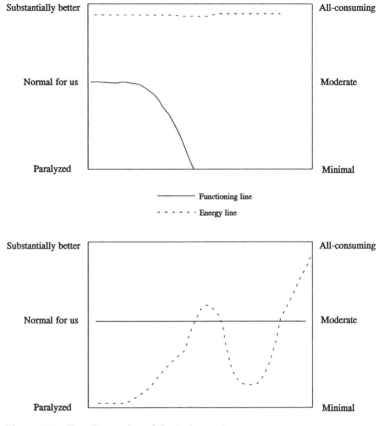

Figure 5.11 Two Examples of the Independent Pattern

flat line, it is unreasonable to expect resource allocation to also resemble a flat line. Most of the energy patterns in the no change group looked as if they belonged in the roller-coaster group. This chart told us that our working hypothesis that resource allocation would be the inverse of the response pattern was correct in most cases.

Timing of Resource Allocation

While doing this analysis, we noticed some variations in the timing of the application of resources. Some families appeared to

Table 5.5 Energy Patterns and Functioning Patterns

	Reciprocal Pattern		Parallel Pattern		Independent Pattern		Total
	No.	%	No.	%	No.	%	No.
Decreased	3	75	0	0	1	25	4
Roller Coaster	33	75	5	11	6	14	44
Mixed	3	43	3	43	1	14	7
No Change	0	0	1	7	14	93	15
Increased	6	50	3	25	3	25	12
Total	45	55	12	15	25	31	82

	Reciprocal Pattern	Other Patterns	Total
Negative Patterns	39	16	55
Positive Patterns	6	21	27
Total	45	37	82

$\chi^2 = 17.348$
Significant at .001 level

expend a great deal of time, effort, and energy early in their stressful experience. In many cases, energy expenditure jumped immediately almost to the all-consuming point on the charts. It remained high in the initial period and then dropped off as family functioning improved. It appeared in these cases that energy expenditure was driving family functioning.

Other families waited until functioning decreased and then reacted. These families invested time, effort, and energy in response to problems, and they invested only what was necessary to handle the problems. It appeared that the functioning drove the resource allocation. Wanting to know then whether the timing of resource allocation was associated with positive and negative patterns of family functioning, we created Table 5.6.

The table shows a marked difference between the roller-coaster and increased groups and very small numbers in the other groups in early or late application of resources. Twenty-six of 42 individuals (62%) in the roller-coaster group expended time, effort, and

Table 5.6 Timing of the Application of Energy to Stressor

	Early	Late	Total
Roller Coaster	16	26	42
Decreased	1	3	4
Mixed	4	3	7
No Change	5	8	13
Increased	11	5	16
Total	37	45	82
	Early	Late	Total
Roller Coaster	16	26	42
Increased	11	5	16
Total	27	31	58

$$\chi^2 = 4.4982$$
Significant at the .05 level

energy later in the process in reaction to the stress. Eleven of 16 individuals (69%) in the increased group applied their efforts earlier in the process. These differences were statistically significant. That could be an indication that time spent denying the problem or devastated and paralyzed is harmful. Accepting the problem early and dealing with it quickly are helpful.

SUMMARY

This chapter focused on the question of the universality of the roller-coaster response pattern developed by Koos (1946). Our data found five different patterns in the way families respond to stress. We found no significant relationship between the type of stressful situation and the response patterns, which indicates that these five patterns might apply to a wide variety of stressful experiences. In addition, we found no gender differences in the patterns. At this point, we are not willing to say that gender differences do not exist—only that we did not find them in our data.

Our research indicates that the way a family defines the seriousness of its situation is related to which model it experiences. The roller-coaster model is associated with the highest levels of seriousness reported by the families. The increased model is related to the lowest reported levels. We do not indicate the direction the relationships might run, but further research might show that certain strong families define their problems less seriously than other families and make themselves impervious to the negative ups and downs of stress.

The findings in this chapter have several implications for practitioners and researchers. The implications will be discussed in Chapter 10.

Variation Within the Family System

The previous chapter dealt with the ways the overall family functioning changes during stress, but it did not deal with the question of whether different aspects of family systems respond in different or unique ways to stress. This chapter examines our data for insights about this question. We gathered data about the ways nine specific aspects of family systems changed as the families managed the six different stressful situations.

This issue is important because it is possible that some aspects of family systems may respond differently during times of stress. Some aspects of family systems may tend to improve, at least under certain circumstances. Others may be impaired, and some may not tend to change in a systematic manner. Also, different kinds of stress may lead to different patterns of change in specific aspects of family systems. For example, couples who are unable to conceive a child may find that marital satisfaction is usually disrupted but that daily routines and chores tend to be unaffected. On the other hand, the stress of having a chronically ill child may have a predictable effect on chores and routines but not influence marital satisfaction. And some aspects of family systems may have considerable variation in the ways they respond to stress, while other aspects may have little variation.

We believe the issue this chapter deals with is important in understanding how family life responds to stress; the findings have important implications for practitioners and future research and theory. We also believe that it is not a mere oversight or accident that this issue has not been addressed in previous research. The positivistic approach that has dominated inquiry in the family stress area for the past half century leads to different research questions. It leads to questions about the causes or determinants of the amount of stress rather than understanding the processes that occur during stress. If we also had conducted our research with the previous paradigmatic orientation, this issue probably would not have come up in this project. The research questions addressed in this chapter would not have occurred to us, and the chapter would not exist. Thus the primary contribution of our shift to an indeterministic and systemic epistemology in this chapter is that it created new questions, a new direction of inquiry that led us to look at some of the subsystem processes within family systems.

Because the questions this chapter deals with have not been asked in previous research about family stress, we had no basis for speculating or hypothesizing about how specific parts of family systems would evolve and change during stress. Thus this chapter is exploratory and breaking new ground.

METHODOLOGY

To begin, we identified different aspects of the family system and tried to define each of the nine areas in ways that could be easily communicated to the families we wanted to interview. We used the following definitions:

- *marital satisfaction*, or feelings about a spouse and happiness within the relationship;
- *rituals and celebrations*, including Christmas, birthdays, anniversaries, Mother's Day, vacations, and so on;
- *leadership*, or the executive function—running things, having control, making decisions, and being in charge;
- *family development*, or moving along life's course by bearing, rearing, and launching children;
- *daily routines and chores*, including mealtime, bedtime, cleanup, dishes, habitual tasks, and family activities;
- *emotional climate*, including strong negative feelings such as sadness, anger, hurt, tension (increased negative feelings were considered a disrupted emotional climate);

- *cohesion and togetherness*, represented as pulling together, connectedness, loyalty, caring, and being united;
- *communication*, or willingness to spend time talking, sharing ideas, open or closed communication patterns, actively listening rather than always speaking, actively seeking others' ideas, tapping into others' true emotions, and empathizing; and
- *contention*, or fighting, arguing, yelling, animosity, and resentment (increased frequency or severity indicates disruption).

There are, of course, many other aspects of family systems on which we also could have focused. We spent considerable time discussing which areas we ought to include; at one time we had some 20 areas. Gradually, we concluded that focusing on a larger number of areas would probably detract from our ability to get other desired data. We therefore reduced our inquiry to these nine subsystems. We had little basis in the literature for deciding which areas would be the most meaningful or important. We decided to include marital satisfaction because it is studied so extensively and there is such a widespread interest in the topic. Most of the other areas are also aspects of considerable interest in the field. For example, family rituals have become major areas of theory, research, and intervention in recent years (Steinglass et al., 1987), and family development has a long history of importance (Duvall, 1955; Falicov, 1988).

The data for this part of the study were collected from a series of charts constructed by each respondent. During the interviews the respondents were asked whether nine different aspects of their family lives changed during their stressful situations. They were shown a grid for each specific area such as the one in Figure 6.1. They were then asked to identify when their stresses began and to describe what happened to each specific aspect of their families.

For example, so we could identify how marital satisfaction changed during stressful periods, the subjects were asked questions such as, "Did your marital satisfaction change during the period when you were experiencing the stress? If it did, how did it change?" Respondents then were shown the blank grid with the label "Marital Satisfaction" above it. Respondents marked the time periods specific to their own situations across the bottom of the grid and then indicated whether their marital satisfaction increased or

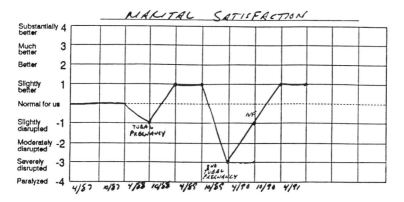

Figure 6.1 Changes in Marital Satisfaction for a Husband Coping With Infertility

decreased from the "normal for us" level they experienced before the stressful situation. Respondents' choices were to indicate whether marital satisfaction was "better," "remained unchanged," or "disrupted." Figure 6.1 is an example of a marital satisfaction chart from a male respondent who was experiencing the stress of infertility. This process was repeated for each aspect of the family system.

Each individual completed his or her chart; we then discussed the charts with the differences and similarities in the subjects' responses and why they responded as they did. The discussion led to insights about how some husbands and wives perceived their situations differently. Also, in some situations the discussion led to individuals wanting to change their chart because the discussion helped them think about events and change they had not thought about before. We let the individuals make changes based on their discussion because our goal was to try to get the most comprehensive and accurate information, and we believed that the discussion helped them think more deeply about aspects of the family situation that they might not have remembered when working alone.

After the data were gathered, we began the rather complex process of trying to find patterns and differences. We had a large number of charts as we assessed nine areas for the 46 families and 82 individuals. Some of the interviews were interrupted or individuals did not want to complete this part of the discussion, but we still had a total of 669 charts to sort and evaluate.

To begin the analysis, the charts were number-coded by the type of stressor and color-coded according to each of the nine aspects. The charts then were grouped according to color or aspect for easier analysis. Each color was laid out on a large table, dividing the aspect into the six stressor groups. Then, each stressor group was examined and subgrouped according to similarity of observed patterns.

MULTIPLE PATTERNS OF RESPONSE

Initially, we identified 16 patterns in the way families responded. Distinctions were made using three criteria:

1. the initial direction of family functioning;
2. the level of functioning following the initial rise or drop; that is, whether functioning rebounded after an initial drop or dropped after an initial rise; and
3. the level of functioning, distinguishing those that were at, below, or above the "normal for us" line on the chart.

As we tried to work with the 16 response patterns, we gradually concluded that it was too large a number and overly detailed. We then tried to group these patterns into slightly more inclusive and general patterns. There were 5 patterns among the 16 that showed initial decreases in functioning and subsequent rebounding. Even though the differences among these five patterns showed varied amounts of rebounding as well as different levels of functioning, these patterns were more alike than different. We grouped them into a more inclusive category that involves a decline and recovery, and called it the *Koos roller-coaster response pattern.*

A similar process was used to condense the other 11 specific patterns into slightly broader categories. Even though our analysis was conducted independently of the initial analysis in Chapter 5, the more general patterns we detected were very similar to the patterns the other members of our research team found as reported in that chapter. We therefore grouped our patterns into the same four categories: roller-coaster, increased, decreased, and no change. We combined the mixed pattern of Chapter 5 with the roller-coaster pattern.

After the other group shared its initial analysis with our research group and we shared our initial analysis, the entire research team discussed whether it would be desirable to use the same typologies in these two chapters or whether we should use the five types in Chapter 5 and the four types in Chapter 6. Eventually, we decided that a similar typology would be best and that it would be useful to have the five types. We then separated out those who had an initial increase and called them "mixed" for consistency with the typology in Chapter 5.

We were impressed with the similarity of the typologies that were developed independently as we and the other group examined the data. We came up with an almost identical typology, and neither group saw the other's working charts or talked with the other during the initial analysis. We believe that this corroboration argues for the validity of the idea that the resulting typology of patterns is consistent and meaningful.

Our focus then turned to the analysis of the response patterns with regard to the nine aspects of family systems. In this analysis, we were working with a smaller number of charts: 69 for marital satisfaction and 75 for each of the other aspects. This made it easier to do the analysis, but we cannot be as conclusive or generalize as much. Table 6.1 is a summary of the percentage of the charts that fit within each response pattern. The table also simplifies the analysis by ignoring the differences in the six different stressors. The differences by stressor are analyzed later in the chapter.

The totals at the bottom of the chart are very informative. The totals for the percentage columns are averages, and they show that the roller-coaster pattern appeared 55% of the time in a look at the specific aspects of the family systems. The increased pattern appeared 13% of the time, no change 11%, mixed 13%, and decreased 7% of the time. Again, these percentages are fairly similar to those found by our group working with Chapter 5, but these were derived with a different type of analysis. The similarity adds credence to the idea that the Koos model should not be viewed as *the* way that families respond to stress. The story has not yet been told

Table 6.1 Response Patterns by Family Aspect, Combining All Stressors

	Roller Coaster		Increased		No Change		Mixed		Decreased	
	No.	%	No.	%	No.	%	No.	%	No.	%
Marital Satisfaction	36	52	12	17	8	12	12	17	1	1
Chores	51	68	6	8	5	7	3	4	10	13
Emotions	63	84	1	1	2	3	7	9	2	3
Cohesion	31	41	22	29	2	3	15	20	5	7
Communication	33	44	22	29	3	4	16	21	1	1
Leadership	29	39	12	16	26	35	7	9	1	1
Rituals	41	55	8	9	8	9	8	9	10	13
Development	41	55	5	7	11	15	7	9	11	15
Contention	45	60	2	3	9	12	15	20	4	5
Totals	370	55	90	13	74	11	90	13	45	7

N = 669 charts (approximately 9 per respondent).

of the other 45% of the respondents who reacted to stress in ways that are different from what the literature would have predicted. Although the other 45% is distributed over four other pattern types, these patterns are nonetheless legitimate and real responses to stress in these particular families. When we combine the percentages for the increased and mixed columns, we see that 26% of these families experienced an initial improvement in functioning across all nine aspects. Although half of these 26% (the mixed pattern) later regressed in their functioning levels, the other half (increased) continued to show improved functioning after the onset of the stressor event.

This information appears to be meaningful because it is not generally thought that families respond to stress in such a manner. It is even more meaningful when we realize that this variation is present even in the small population we studied. It is also important to notice that 11% of the responses in this sample represented no change in functioning at all. Like increased and mixed, the no change category is unlike the Koos model. Also, the decreased pattern is not like the Koos model because there is no rebound following the initial drop in functioning. Seven percent of the responses fell into this decreased category.

By comparing the specific aspects of the family systems with these overall percentages, we begin to learn which parts of family systems respond in unique ways to stress. The marital satisfaction, rituals, family development, and contention in families tend to have response patterns that are very similar to the totals at the bottom of Table 6.1. Apparently, these aspects are typical of the general responses to stress, at least for this sample; that is, a little more than half of the families responded in a Koos-like pattern, while the other four patterns divide among the other 45%.

When we look at the emotional climate, we see that this subsystem changes more dramatically. Approximately 85% of the time, the emotional part of family life responds in the roller-coaster pattern. This is substantially more than any of the other eight subsystems. In other words, the functioning of family emotions tends to be disrupted more frequently at the onset of stress. Thus our data suggest that when significant stress occurs in families, the functioning of the emotional climate tends to be disrupted more often than other aspects of family systems.

It also seems worth noting that the emotional climate improved only 1% of the time, and no change was reported only 3% of the time. Thus it appears that the functioning of the emotional climate in the family realm tends to be disrupted more than other aspects under stress. This is consistent with the idea that Beutler, Burr, Bahr, and Herrin (1989) have argued—that the emotional part of the family realm is a central or fundamental part.

The changes in daily routines and chores is in an intermediate category. It has a roller-coaster pattern some two-thirds of the time. However, adding the percentage from the decreased column shows that stress has an initially negative impact on this area approximately three-fourths of the time.

We are not sure why the daily chores tend to be disrupted so frequently. It is possible that routines and chores are more visible and demanding on a daily basis, and when stress occurs it is immediately obvious if chores are disrupted. It also may be that this is an area in which families feel it is acceptable to lower their standards, so it is easy to simply ignore chores for a time. Instead, family members may use their time to try harder to maintain other processes such as good communication and closeness.

The response patterns with cohesion and communication were quite different. These parts of family systems were disrupted less frequently by the commencement of stress. The roller-coaster patterns for cohesion and togetherness occurred only 41% of the time and only 44% of the time for communication. These are substantially lower than the total average of 55%.

These two aspects of family systems not only experienced less disruption in functioning, but also experienced an actual improvement in functioning more than any of the other seven aspects. The increased column shows that 29% of the respondents indicated that functioning increased in both of these two aspects. Also, when we add the percentages showing an increase in the functioning of these parts of the family life we find that half of all respondents reported an initial increase in functioning. The percentages in the mixed column are 20% for cohesion and togetherness and 21% for communication. Thus our data suggest that approximately half of the families tend to pull together more, with family members talking and listening to one another better when they encounter stressful experiences. This is a silver lining that comes with family stress that has not been documented before; as it becomes more widely known, it may help families maintain higher morale during stressful periods. This may actually contribute to the ability that families have to manage stress more effectively.

The most notable characteristic of the leadership and decision-making aspect of family systems was the small percentage (39%) in the roller-coaster column and the large percentage (35%) in the no change column. These data suggest that the executive subsystem in families tends to change the least, positively or negatively, when stress occurs. Apparently, the way families make decisions and carry out their leadership functions is more insulated from stress when compared with the other aspects of family systems. The response by a husband in a family struggling with infertility illustrates this idea: "I think it was pretty normal throughout. It was pretty much a joint management of the family. If anything, we probably even talked more during the stress of trying to conceive a child."

THE ROLE OF STRESSOR TYPE AND GENDER

Next we turned to a more detailed analysis of the response patterns. We wanted to see if there were differences in the responses in the six different types of stressor. We also wanted to examine the responses to determine if there were discernable gender differences. The findings again deal with questions that have never been raised in the field before, and they provide several important new insights into family processes. This analysis divides the data into small units, so it is important to remain appropriately tentative about the conclusions. Thus in this part of our analysis the findings are more suggestive and indicative than conclusive, and there is a greater need for additional research to try to replicate the findings.

It could be argued that the number of cases is so small in some parts of this analysis that we should not include this section in our findings. However, the fact that there are small numbers and zeros in some of the cells is important because the variation even in a small sample provides several previously unknown insights into family processes. The new insights have such far-reaching implications for practitioners that, even though some of them are very tentative, we believe it is important to publish them; future research projects that replicate these findings can determine which patterns are worth attending to and which are not.

Marital Satisfaction

Table 6.2 shows the way marital satisfaction changed in each of the six stressful situations. Several differences seem noteworthy. In the bankruptcy group, 83% of the response patterns were a typical Koos-like roller coaster, whereas only 33% of the muscular dystrophy, infertility, and displaced homemaker groups experienced the roller-coaster pattern.

One possible reason for these differences could be that marital satisfaction may be more directly connected to bankruptcy than the other three stressors. Bankruptcy can often be blamed on the actions of one or both marriage partners, while problems such as dystrophy and infertility are medical problems and less attributable to the actions of either parent. If one parent or the other can be blamed for such a major stressor, then it seems logical that marital satisfaction would be more closely related. This is illustrated by a comment made by one of the wives in a bankruptcy situation: "I've instigated a lot of the blaming and anger at him when it's not his fault."

On the other hand, dystrophy, infertility, and being displaced are more attacks on the family rather than on the spouse. As such, they become common enemies and require spouses' cooperation. Such cooperation may actually help the marital relationship in many situations and also help satisfy some of the spouses' needs. A father in his 60s whose adopted son developed muscular dystrophy explained.

"It's brought us all together as a team: very, very close. We're all together. Probably Marc [the child with muscular dystrophy], because of his condition, made us better people. You know what I'm saying? Instead of just going through the regular life, we have to plan out and have to think out things. You know, where you move,

Table 6.2 Marital Satisfaction Response Patterns by Type of Stressor

	Roller Coaster No.	%	Increased No.	%	No Change No.	%	Mixed No.	%	Decreased No.	%	Total No.
Bankruptcy	10	83	2	16	0	0	0	0	0	0	12
Institutionalized Child	9	75	0	0	2	15	2	15	0	0	13
Muscular Dystrophy	6	33	5	27	5	27	2	11	0	0	18
Infertility	6	33	3	16	1	5	8	44	0	0	18
Troubled Teen	4	80	1	20	0	0	0	0	0	0	5
Displaced Homemaker	1	33	1	33	0	0	0	0	1	33	3
Total	36	52	12	17	8	12	12	17	1	1	69

having to make changes in the home, having to put a ramp here, or little things like that. They're not really disruptions, but we're more thoughtful because everybody has to be considered. Marital satisfaction . . . I think this is one of the things that keeps a marriage together is people having to do and share things together."

Sixty percent of the infertility patterns showed an initial rise above the normal-for-us line; that is, functioning was better. This is illustrated in the following comment by the husband of a couple experiencing infertility.

"I think that we've just gotten closer and more caring for each other and more in tune and stronger in our marriage. I don't think that I could ever say that the marriage has ever been disrupted. The other things are disrupted, but the marriage part of it has not been. Today, I would say that we're a lot better off than we were starting."

However, most of those with an initial rise later declined to either a normal-for-us or a disrupted level of functioning. It is also interesting that more than half of the couples coping with dystrophy felt their marriage was better during the stressful situation. On the other hand, few marriages were better when couples were struggling with teenagers and an institutionalized child. Thus it appears that the way marital satisfaction develops while families are coping with stress depends somewhat on the nature of the stress.

We divided the charts by gender to discern gender differences in the patterns. There was variation within both genders, but the patterns and percentages based on gender were not discernible.

Daily Routines and Chores

The data for routines and chores are in Table 6.3. This table shows that all of the 13 respondents in the institutionalized and handicapped child stressor category reported a roller-coaster response pattern for routines and chores.

The respondents' comments suggest that family routines become severely disrupted until the child is placed in an institution. After that, the burden on the family is reduced and the functioning level is permitted to rebound, as indicated in the following quote

Table 6.3 Daily Routines and Chores Response Patterns by Type of Stressor

	Roller Coaster		Increased		No Change		Mixed		Decreased		Total
	No.	%	No.	%	No.	%	No.	%	No.	%	No.
Bankruptcy	10	83	1	8	1	8	0	0	0	0	12
Institutionalized Child	13	100	0	0	0	0	0	0	0	0	13
Muscular Dystrophy	9	47	1	5	0	0	1	5	8	42	19
Infertility	11	61	2	11	1	5	2	11	2	11	18
Troubled Teen	3	50	1	16	2	33	0	0	0	0	6
Displaced Homemaker	5	71	1	14	1	14	0	0	0	0	7
Total	51	68	6	8	5	7	3	4	10	13	75

by the mother of an institutionalized handicapped girl: "It was very, very hard at first when she was placed, and then as the years went by we started learning how to function again as a family."

A large number of the families coping with bankruptcy, displaced homemaker status, and infertility also experienced a Koos-like response to stress for routines and chores. A possible explanation is that these families found it necessary to spend significant amounts of time away from home and away from usual routines in work or educational situations. A couple trying to conceive a child explained the time required away from home to facilitate all of the medical work.

"The medical tests and procedures are so extensive and time-consuming that it makes it pretty difficult to keep any kind of routine in the family. And, with infertility, you're obligated to go do the procedures at the 'right time of the month,' even on weekends, and it's usually not convenient."

The families with dystrophy showed a larger percentage of permanent disruption in the daily routines and chores. Because muscular dystrophy is a progressive deterioration of the muscle system, these families found it necessary to spend an increasing amount of time caring for their affected children, and apparently it was the routine and chores part of the system that suffered.

We also examined the data to try to detect gender differences with this aspect of family systems. As with the marital satisfaction, however, no meaningful gender differences were found.

Emotional Climate

Of all the areas we studied, the emotional climate showed the highest percentage (84%) of families with a roller-coaster response pattern. This is not too surprising because people commonly describe their emotional experiences as being "like a roller coaster." These data suggest that the emotional climate is the most volatile, up-and-down aspect of the family system. The mother of a boy with muscular dystrophy illustrated this volatility:

"It's below normal, for me. Well, this is when he went through the testing. It was a very emotional time. It didn't go away for a while. I was always on an emotional roller coaster, and it had to have influenced the family. Then, towards the end it got worse."

Adding the 3% from the decreased column we find that 87% of all families in the study experienced an initial drop in functioning of the emotional climate aspect. Although stress may not be too disruptive to some of the other aspects, it appears to take a toll on the emotional climate almost all of the time:

"We had gotten to the point where we had our son in the hospital for nearly a month and we had no clue that this was it [before they found out what he had] and at that point that we found out that the kid . . . had muscular dystrophy, it was totally paralyzing; to the point that there was no work, there was nothing, no operation. And, of course, you got to the point where you slowly, gradually bring your emotions back to normal. And then as you come to these sign posts [worsening changes in a child's condition], your emotions are slightly disrupted or moderately disrupted. We had a real hard time with the wheelchair—I remember when we finally decided that Jeremy had gotten to the point where he couldn't wear his braces anymore and we had to get a wheelchair, and that was severely disruptive to me. In fact, I remember saying to him, *'You* are gonna walk!' and he said, 'But Dad, I can't.' And at that point—remember when he sat out in the hallway—and I said, 'Just walk! Do you want to get in the wheelchair?' and he said, 'I don't, but I can't.' And, at that point it was pretty disruptive. Our emotional climate was pretty rough.

"We actually functioned as a family but we didn't function — kind of functioned in a helter-skelter manner and then you go back to when we put him in braces—the same emotional feelings—kinda to the point where you almost put it out of your head, 'Well, maybe they'll find a cure'—like in any feeling. I guess the stages of acceptance in a terminal disease, each stage that you go through—if you put them in braces or put them in a wheelchair, your emotions and your family's functioning and everything that you consider as a family unit does not operate as well."

As we look at the specific stressors in Table 6.4 interacting with emotional climate, we find that the Koos model provides a very accurate description of what is happening in these families. For example, the roller-coaster types were seen in 92% (11 of 12) of the bankruptcy charts, 92% (12 of 13) of the institutionalized child charts, 79% (15 of 19) of the terminally ill child charts, 67% (12 of 18) of the infertility charts, 100% (6 of 6) of the troubled teen charts, and 86% (6 of 7) of the displaced homemaker charts.

Another aspect of the changes in the emotional climate is that the emotional aspect does not simply decrease and remain there. This only happened 3% of the time. Thus the emotional part of family life tends to be disrupted the most readily and dramatically, but families tend to recover from the disruption one way or another. The mother of a troubled teen described how the emotional climate did improve.

"I would say it didn't feel very good to be here in the home. It was better to be somewhere else at that time. The climate was just like heavy and tense and thick. . . . It is slightly better than normal now. It's a fun place to be, it's relaxing. It feels like home and it feels normal, and sometimes we're just very happy as a family. There's still fighting and contention, but it generally feels very comfortable and peaceful to be here."

Thus the Koos model seems to be the best description of what happens to the emotional part of families when stress is high, and this tends to be the same regardless of the type of stress.

We suspected that if gender differences were to appear with any of the areas, then they would probably be the most likely to appear with this area. Again, however, there was variation within both men and women, although we were not able to detect any meaningful differences between them. This same pattern appeared with each of the other nine areas.

Togetherness and Cohesion

There is considerable variation in togetherness and cohesion in the different stressors. With bankruptcy, there is usually a roller-coaster pattern. With dystrophy, institutionalized children, and infertility, however, the patterns are quite different. With dystrophy a permanent increase in cohesion is seen more than half the time; it occurs one-third of the time with troubled teens. There is an initial increase in cohesion more than two-thirds of the time with the

Table 6.4 Emotional Climate Response Patterns by Type of Stressor

| | Roller Coaster | | Increased | | No Change | | Mixed | | Decreased | | Total |
	No.	%	No.	%	No.	%	No.	%	No.	%	No.
Bankruptcy	12	100	0	0	0	0	0	0	0	0	12
Institutionalized Child	12	92	0	0	0	0	0	0	1	8	13
Muscular Dystrophy	15	79	1	5	2	10	0	0	1	5	19
Infertility	12	67	0	0	0	0	6	33	0	0	18
Troubled Teen	6	100	0	0	0	0	0	0	0	0	6
Displaced Homemaker	6	86	0	0	0	0	1	14	0	0	7
Total	63	84	1	1	2	3	7	9	2	3	75

institutionalized child; with 46% of the families it is followed by a roller-coaster pattern. (See Table 6.5.)

Of interest is the fact that these three stressors—where there is the most increase in cohesion—all deal with small children or the lack of desired children. It seems that stress seems to do as much to improve togetherness and cohesion as to hurt it—at least initially. Apparently, as families try to meet and manage stress, about half of the time they tend to "come together," at least at first. Comments from two couples seeking help for infertility confirm this insight.

First Couple

HUSBAND: When you're first finding out about things [medical reasons for infertility] you're really not together yet. It takes a while to sort that out.

WIFE: You're more worried about yourself. You're trying to sort your sexuality and what's happening to your body before you get [pregnant] so it's a joint thing against it [infertility]. Now it's us against infertility. . . . It's a couple thing.

Second Couple

WIFE: Actually, through the infertility, the togetherness went higher because of the support. We were already close, but it brought us closer together.

Communication

Communication may be the aspect of family systems most benefited by the onset of major stress. Twenty-nine percent of the respondents reported a permanent increase in communication patterns, and 21% showed early increases with later variations in levels. Thus 50% of the families initially increased in functioning in this aspect. Also, of all the aspects studied, the communication part of family systems had the most charts finishing above the normal functioning line; in fact, 67% of the time communication was actually better than before. (See Table 6.6.)

Table 6.5 Togetherness and Cohesion Response Patterns by Type of Stressor

	Roller Coaster No.	%	Increased No.	%	No Change No.	%	Mixed No.	%	Decreased No.	%	Total No.
Bankruptcy	9	75	2	17	0	0	0	0	1	8	12
Institutionalized Child	4	31	3	23	0	0	6	46	0	0	13
Muscular Dystrophy	4	21	10	53	1	5	1	5	3	16	19
Infertility	7	39	3	17	0	0	7	37	1	6	18
Troubled Teen	4	67	2	33	0	0	0	0	0	0	6
Displaced Homemaker	3	43	2	29	1	14	1	14	0	0	7
Total	31	41	22	29	2	3	15	20	5	7	75

Considerable evidence thus exists that communication tends to improve when stress occurs in family systems. It could be that family members seem to know that they must communicate more frequently and more effectively. In times of mutual difficulty family members also may tend to listen better. The mother of an institutionalized handicapped child illustrates this finding:

"We don't just talk about things we used to talk about. We talk about how we feel more and our fears, just deeper conversations. We talk about life and afterlife and death and love and, you know, more than we used to. It was never a subject we talked about before. It makes you think through a lot of things you never thought about before. You have to."

A displaced homemaker and mother of two also illustrated this finding:

"I have really found that after some tragedies that have happened that I have got to put our family first, and really sit and listen and communicate, and put all of the family problems as number one. And then all of the other problems will balance out and work out."

Substantial differences also were seen in the different kinds of stress. The communication with displaced homemakers tended to follow a roller-coaster pattern. At the other extreme, the roller-coaster pattern was least frequent with families struggling with infertility and troubled teens. The communication improved two thirds of the time with the troubled teen group. Some of the reasons for this probably include eliminating poor communication patterns and increased focus on improving communication in most therapy programs.

Family Leadership and Decision Making

The two general conclusions about leadership are (a) the roller-coaster pattern occurred less often with this aspect than any of the aspects and (b) this aspect of family systems had the most no change type of functioning. (See Table 6.7.)

A few differences were found between the various stressors. The roller-coaster pattern was least evident with the institutionalized

Table 6.6 Communication Response Patterns by Type of Stressor

	Roller Coaster		Increased		No Change		Mixed		Decreased		Total
	No.	%	No.	%	No.	%	No.	%	No.	%	No.
Bankruptcy	6	50	4	33	0	0	2	17	0	0	12
Institutionalized Child	6	46	5	38	0	0	2	15	0	0	13
Muscular Dystrophy	8	42	4	21	3	16	3	16	1	5	19
Infertility	5	28	4	22	0	0	9	50	0	0	18
Troubled Teen	2	33	4	67	0	0	0	0	0	0	6
Displaced Homemaker	6	86	1	14	0	0	0	0	0	0	7
Total	33	44	22	29	3	4	16	21	1	1	75

Table 6.7 Leadership and Decision-Making Response Patterns by Type of Stressor

| | Roller Coaster | | Increased | | No Change | | Mixed | | Decreased | | Total |
	No.	%	No.	%	No.	%	No.	%	No.	%	No.
Bankruptcy	6	50	1	8	5	42	0	0	0	0	12
Institutionalized Child	3	23	4	31	4	31	2	15	0	0	13
Muscular Dystrophy	5	26	4	21	8	42	2	11	0	0	19
Infertility	9	50	1	6	4	22	3	17	1	6	18
Troubled Teen	2	33	1	17	3	50	0	0	0	0	6
Displaced Homemaker	4	57	1	14	2	29	0	0	0	0	7
Total	29	39	12	16	26	35	7	9	1	1	75

child and dystrophy families. It only occurred approximately one-fourth of the time. Also, in the three areas where the roller-coaster pattern occurred least, there were more who experienced an improvement in the functioning of the executive subsystem. There also were differences in the families who experienced no change. In approximately half of the families dealing with troubled teens, bankruptcy, and muscular dystrophy, there was no change.

Family Rituals and Celebrations

The families experiencing three of the six stressors had particularly high percentages of those who experienced a roller-coaster pattern in rituals and celebrations: families with bankruptcy, institutionalized children, and infertility. (See Table 6.8.)

We suspect that the frequent occurrence of the roller-coaster pattern with bankruptcy is a reflection of the lack of ready cash for nonessential items such as vacations, birthday and Christmas gifts, and anniversaries. Referring to family rituals and celebrations, a husband who had experienced bankruptcy reported, "It disrupted things probably because of our concerns about money."

The institutionalized and handicapped child category had 85% of the Koos-like responses. Possible explanations are:

- the financial costs of an institutionalized child are heavy;
- many parents often have to travel long distances to be with their institutionalized children;
- such children are often immobile, which presents particular concerns with, for example, family vacations;
- disruptions of the children's routines; and
- buying appropriate gifts and toys is often difficult.

The following comments illustrate these issues.

"It's hard on family outings knowing someone is missing. . . . We go visit him on holidays. Bringing him here makes him unhappy because it upsets his routine so much so we just go there."

"We didn't go on vacation for about three years. . . . At Christmastime everybody was just so upset about everything, and as years have gone by it's just not the same. It's really difficult, because we

Table 6.8 Family Rituals and Celebrations Response Patterns by Type of Stressor

	Roller Coaster No.	Roller Coaster %	Increased No.	Increased %	No Change No.	No Change %	Mixed No.	Mixed %	Decreased No.	Decreased %	Total No.
Bankruptcy	11	92	0	0	0	0	0	0	1	8	12
Institutionalized Child	11	85	1	8	0	0	0	0	1	8	13
Muscular Dystrophy	5	26	6	32	2	11	1	5	5	26	19
Infertility	10	56	1	6	0	0	5	28	2	11	18
Troubled Teen	1	17	0	0	5	83	0	0	0	0	6
Displaced Homemaker	3	43	0	0	1	14	2	29	1	14	7
Total	41	55	8	9	8	9	8	9	10	13	75

bring her in her wheelchair. It's a constant reminder to them. . . . It's always hard on the rituals, because with normal children you've got it all planned and it's really easy, but with handicapped kids, the presents are really hard to buy. At Christmas time, it seems like it's hardest. I used to love Christmas. It was my favorite time of year. I go through a terrible, terrible time, don't I?"

"I remember one time going to a store, and a lady was complaining that she didn't know what to buy her 3-year-old granddaughter, and she was looking at all these things. I just started to cry, because Kenzi at the time was 5, and she should have been enjoying her first doll, and I was trying to find toys that not even a 3-month-old could use. It's very, very stressful trying to find something for her, and you want to be joyful for her, but it's not."

The stress of infertility also exhibited a strong roller-coaster pattern: 56% of families reported an initial drop with respect to family rituals and celebrations. Because so many of the traditional family celebrations revolve around children and because none of the couples in our sample had children, it seems logical that family rituals and celebrations will be disrupted for couples who want to have a child. Most of these couples reported particular difficulty with Mother's Day. For many, Mother's Day is not even considered a holiday. One couple, who had been married for nine years, had experienced only one pregnancy that resulted in a stillbirth five days before Christmas. This couple made the following comments.

HUSBAND: So many of the holidays throughout the year are most important when you're celebrating them with your kids. When you don't have your kids with you, it really drove home the point to us that those things that had been important as far as special occasions and so forth really didn't have that specialness anymore.

WIFE: We noticed, too—at Christmastime, I think I probably noticed it more this year than before—that the majority of Christmas songs are almost all singing about or for children. So it's just kind of like you get a little tired of hearing those kind of things. For me, personally, the two worst holidays in my life are Mother's Day and Christmas, because, again, there's such an emphasis on children. Like last year, I had one or two of my relatives [who] sent me Mother's

Day cards anyway to try to make me feel better, saying,
"Well, you're still a mother, because you had this baby for
nine months." It was a very, very difficult thing, and I
would have almost rather not had anything at all. The holidays became worse after having gone through a fertility
procedure and having such a horrible loss.

Another unique pattern is seen in Table 6.8: Considerable variation among the families with dystrophy. About a quarter of them
had the roller-coaster pattern with their rituals. A third of them
found this part of their life improved, and a quarter had a permanent decrease. This rather high variation in how this part of the
family life changed raises a question for future research. Why did
the families with this particular stress have such variation in the
ritual and celebrations aspect of their family system?

Family Development

One of the most significant findings about family development
is that only 7% of the response patterns demonstrate an increase in
family functioning, which is substantially lower than the average
of 13%. This probably results from the simple fact that most of
these stressors tend by their nature to cause family development to
get stuck. Another important finding is that 15% of the respondents reported that family development decreased in functioning.
This percentage is the highest within the decreased column in
Table 6.1. (See also Table 6.9.)

In addition, all of the 15% who had a permanent decrease came
from only two of the six stressor groups: families dealing with terminally ill children and infertility. With the latter, because they
cannot move into the child-rearing stage of the normal family life
cycle, there is considerable disruption of family development. One
wife commented, "As we started finding out, it became more and
more disrupted and it went down a lot further. We stopped making
decisions on how to live our lives and what we did, whether to buy
a four-door car or not or whether to go on a vacation or not. What
we were going to do as a family changed totally, and so I felt that

Table 6.9 Family Development Response Patterns by Type of Stressor

	Roller Coaster No.	%	Increased No.	%	No Change No.	%	Mixed No.	%	Decreased No.	%	Total No.
Bankruptcy	9	75	0	0	3	25	0	0	0	0	12
Institutionalized Child	11	85	1	8	0	0	1	8	0	0	13
Muscular Dystrophy	5	26	4	21	3	16	3	16	4	21	19
Infertility	9	50	0	0	0	0	2	11	7	39	18
Troubled Teen	4	67	0	0	2	33	0	0	0	0	6
Displaced Homemaker	3	43	0	0	3	43	1	14	0	0	7
Total	41	55	5	7	11	15	7	9	11	15	75

it went way down and then after we got a grasp on the situation is when we started coming back up said, 'We're gonna still lead a life that is as normal as we can.' "

The families dealing with muscular dystrophy had a different type of disruption in their family life cycle. They had moved into the child-rearing stage, but with the child tending to regress physically rather than progress, a disruption of the family member along the typical life course. As the child becomes a teenager, he or she is regressing toward infancy in needing physical care. The following conversation illustrates what one father of a handicapped and terminally ill child experienced in terms of family development:

"What you should be doing as your kids get to the elementary school age is, you know, they should be going and having sleep overs with other kids. Then, when they get to be teenagers, they should be doing things that Mike couldn't do. So he started becoming more of an infant at the very time that he should have been becoming more mature. In terms of family development, the other kids kept developing in the normal way. The family as far as they were concerned was pretty normal. But in terms of what we were experiencing, as you go through the years, we kind of went back to having an infant. It wasn't a normal stage of life. It was a reversal that suddenly was eliminated when he died. You can't chart that."

The father of an institutionalized and handicapped daughter reported how his family became stuck for several years: "After she was born, for five years we didn't dare have children because we didn't know if the same results were to come. Our original plans were to have children every two years."

One conclusion that seems to emerge from the data is that the nature of the stressor seems to make more difference in how this aspect of family systems responds to stress than most of the other aspects.

Contention

This is also an aspect of family life in which the nature of the stressor seems to make a difference in what happens. With the troubled teens, each and every family (100%) had a roller-coaster pattern. Also a large percentage of those dealing with bankruptcy and displaced homemakers had a roller-coaster pattern. However, at the other extreme, only one-third of the dystrophy families had a roller-coaster pattern. (See Table 6.10.)

Another interesting tendency in the data is that only 3% of the families experienced an improvement in the contention part of their family system. Apparently, stress increases contention in some situations but rarely improves the situation in families that already have contention in stressful situations. One couple with an institutionalized child reported that family contention decreased when they removed the stress by placing their daughter in an institution for handicapped children.

WIFE: Once the decision was made and once we talked to the kids about that, I think things were a little bit better.

HUSBAND: Yes! There was a burden lifted.

CONCLUSIONS

The data in this chapter provide several new insights into processes that occur in family systems during periods of family stress. The findings in this chapter do not provide insights about what the causes are; we believe that type of effort would be a fruitless search for deterministic laws that do not exist and would not be useful if we invented them. Our goal is to better understand the systemic processes that occur in some of the subsystems in families and the probabilities with which they occur. We hope that the findings lead us in the direction of developing general principles that will be helpful to practitioners. In this chapter, the data seem to justify six moderately general conclusions.

First, the data in this chapter reinforce the conclusion that emerged in Chapter 5 that considerably more variation is seen in the way family systems respond to stress than is generally recognized in the family stress literature. In both chapters we found that the roller-coaster pattern only occurs approximately half the time and that four other patterns are seen in the way the overall functioning of families changes and in the way specific aspects of family systems

Table 6.10 Contention Response Patterns by Type of Stressor

	Roller Coaster		Increased		No Change		Mixed		Decreased		Total
	No.	%	No.	%	No.	%	No.	%	No.	%	No.
Bankruptcy	9	75	0	0	2	17	0	0	1	8	12
Institutionalized Child	7	54	1	8	1	8	4	31	0	0	13
Muscular Dystrophy	6	32	0	0	6	32	5	26	2	11	19
Infertility	11	61	0	0	0	0	6	33	1	6	18
Troubled Teen	6	100	0	0	0	0	0	0	0	0	6
Displaced Homemaker	6	86	1	14	0	0	0	0	0	0	7
Total	45	60	2	3	9	12	15	20	4	5	75

change. Approximately 15% of the time things get better, 10% of the time things do not change, 15% of the time there is a mixed pattern of improvement and then a roller-coaster pattern, and 5% of the time things deteriorate and never recover. We had slightly different ways of getting our data in this chapter, but the findings were remarkably consistent.

Second, the data in this chapter also seem to show that specific aspects of family systems tend to respond in slightly different ways when families encounter stress. The third and fourth conclusions are more specific findings about this second idea.

Third, a silver lining is seen within some of the subsystem processes during family stress. Approximately one-third of the time, as families cope with stress, there is improvement in the quality of their communication and their cohesion. We do not yet know very much about the circumstances that tend to bring this about, but the data are clear that improvement occurs in a sizable number of families. Some improvement tends to occur in several other aspects of family life, but it is less common than with communication and cohesion. Marital satisfaction and the quality of the executive subsystem improves approximately one-sixth of the time. The performance—or routines, rituals, and chores—tends to improve approximately 10% of the time.

Fourth, one aspect of family systems is almost always disrupted when stress occurs: 90% of the time the emotional climate is disturbed. Apparently, the emotional part of the family realm is a sensitive part that responds quickly and predictably to difficulties. The aspect of family systems that is adversely affected next most frequently, approximately 80%, is daily routines and chores.

Fifth, the specific aspects of family systems tend to be more responsive to stress than the overall functioning of the system. We observed that the peaks and valleys of respondents' charted perceptions are more pronounced (higher peaks and lower valleys) for the specific aspects of family systems than the overall family functioning charts described in Chapter 5. Whereas, it seems that respondents may perceive the *overall* family system (see previous chapter) as being relatively resilient and less susceptible to dramatic fluctuation ("Life just goes on!"), they seem to see the smaller parts of the system (specific aspects such as emotional climate or marital satisfaction) as more dramatically affected by the onset of stress.

Sixth, the nature of the stress is often related to the way the specific aspects of family systems respond to stress. For example, when families are coping with infertility and dystrophy, these stressors tend to disrupt the family development more than the other four we studied. The family cohesion is disrupted 83% of the time when families are coping with bankruptcy but only 37% of the time with muscular dystrophy. Contention was universally worse in families with troubled teens, but only decreased half the time when a child was handicapped and institutionalized.

SUMMARY

The purpose of this chapter was to determine whether different aspects of family systems respond in different ways to stress. We focused on nine specific aspects of family systems as we reviewed data collected from families who had experienced six different stressful situations. Overall, the patterns of response were remarkably similar to the patterns reported in Chapter 5. In other words, in addition to the Koos pattern, large variation exists in the way families respond to stress, so four other patterns are useful in describing family responses. Furthermore, we found that some of the subsystems in family systems respond in unique ways to stress. Some subsystems are impaired by, some are improved by, and some are impervious to stress. The most dramatic finding was that the emotional climate in family systems is the most likely to be disrupted during periods of stress. Approximately 85% of the time, the emotional subsystem tends to be disrupted. It is rare to have no change in the emotional climate and almost unheard of to have this part of family systems improve during stress. Four of the areas we studied responded predictably in a Koos-like fashion 50% to 60% of the time: marital satisfaction, rituals, family development, and contention. The amount of cohesion and quality of the communication in families were dramatically different. They were disrupted approximately one-third of the time, but they actually improved almost one-fourth of the time. Finally, the leadership aspect seems to change least of all. It seems rather impervious to stress. We also discovered that the subsystems in families tend to be more responsive to stress than the system as a whole.

The nature of the stressful input also appears to be related to how specific parts of the family system change. Stressors that tend to be inside the family system, such as infertility and severe illness, tend to disrupt the growth and development of the family and its day-to-day functioning. Stressors that come from outside the family, such as bankruptcy, have a stronger negative influence on cohesion. Families with troubled teens all reported that contention was much worse for them. These findings are suggestive at best, but they illustrate the complexity of family responses to stress even within a limited sample. Further replication and study is needed with other types of stressors and with different types of populations.

In terms of gender differences, there appear to be fewer differences than we suspected, at least with regard to differential responses to specific aspects of the family system. Men and women both reported variation, but we could not find differences that were accounted for by being male or female. Other populations may yield different results, so gender differences remain an intriguing area of study.

The findings in this chapter have several implications for family practitioners. These are discussed in Chapter 10.

SEVEN

Reconceptualizing Coping Strategies

McCubbin (1979) introduced the concept of coping strategies; it is now a central concept in the family stress literature. However, some confusion persists in the use of this concept stemming from scholars' inconsistent use and definition of the concepts of resources, correlates, and coping strategies. For example, many of the factors that are now being identified in the literature as coping strategies are not strategies. They are merely correlates of how well families deal with stress.

The purpose of this chapter is to help clarify the differences between these three concepts and then examine the literature on coping strategies to develop a more coherent conceptual framework. This chapter was written in the early stages of the research project, and we then used it as the conceptual framework for our research about the circumstances under which various coping strategies are helpful and harmful.

RESOURCES, CORRELATES, AND COPING STRATEGIES

Boss (1987) was the first scholar to distinguish between resources and coping strategies:

At first glance, family coping appears to operationalize Hill's B factor (family resources), but the concept is, in fact, a unique dimension that is not accommodated by Hill's original ABC-X model. . . . The family's coping resources are its individual and collective strengths at the time the stressor event occurs. Examples are economic security, health, intelligence, job skills, proximity, spirit of cooperation, relationship skills, and network and social supports. The family's resources, therefore, are the sociological, economic, psychological, emotional, and physical assets on which the members can draw in response to a single stressor event or an accumulation of events. However, having resources does not imply how the family will use them. For example, a family may use a resource such as money to cope with the event of unemployment in a maladaptive way (e.g., to buy more liquor) or more functionally (e.g., to look for another job). Thus, the availability and the amount of family resources remain static (no process) variables that can be rather easily assessed by researchers and therapists. (Boss, 1987, p. 702)

In other words, what a family has available to it and what family members actually think, feel, and do with these resources are two very different ideas. Thus *family coping strategies* should be defined as the active processes and behaviors families actually try to do to help them manage, adapt, or deal with the stressful situation (McCubbin & Dahl, 1985). *Family resources* are the characteristics or strengths a family has at its disposal.

A sizable body of literature also has identified factors that correlate with how well families deal with stress. The very first study of family stress is an example of this type of research. In his study of how 50 families reacted to the Depression of the 1930s, Angell (1936) asked what "sorts of qualities are significant in determining how the family as a socio-psychological unit will react to the decrease? The answer [that] serious study of these 50 cases seems to give is: Integration and Adaptability" (Angell, 1936, p. 14).

Thus integration and adaptability were identified as the two main factors that correlated with how well families adjusted to the Depression. This study did not try to determine whether it was helpful for families to have more integrated or more adaptable coping strategies. All we know from Angell's study and other correlational studies is that families who are relatively more adaptable or more integrated tend to adjust more effectively than families who are less adaptable or integrated.

Scholars in the field seem to believe that it is defensible to make inferences about coping strategies from the research studies about correlates, but it is important to realize that this is a sizable inferential leap that should be viewed tentatively because it is using mere correlations that have been acquired in cross-sectional methods as the basis for making inferences about processes in family systems. The inference is made in the following way: Because high adaptability and high integration tend to be associated with effectively managing the stressful situation, it follows that if families try to be more adaptable or more integrated, then these strategies will probably help them adjust more effectively. Actually, these correlational studies only provide a meager basis for this inference, and it is probably essential that we add the qualification that the conclusion is only relevant for families who were previously low in adaptability and integration; that is, it is probably only families who are low in adaptability and integration that benefit from trying to be more adaptable or integrated.

Distinguishing resources, correlates, and coping strategies from one another is important for several reasons. Most of the literature that has focused on resources and correlates was a positivistic search for determinants of family disorganization. The introduction of coping strategies was an attempt to move toward a different epistemological and pragmatic approach. It was an attempt to introduce a systemic perspective and to try to develop ideas that had more value to practitioners. Being aware of these differences helps us know when we are thinking deterministically and when we are thinking systemically. It also helps us be more aware of how much supporting evidence we have for some of the suggested coping strategies. Although the correlational studies are useful in helping us know which factors warrant further study, we need a different type of research that focuses on how helpful strategies really are when they are purposefully used by a family rather than merely correlates.

TOWARD A CONCEPTUAL FRAMEWORK
OF COPING STRATEGIES

The current family science literature has several different lists of coping strategies. Some of these lists are relatively long and sometimes are presented side by side. For example, in their analysis of family stress, McCubbin and Dahl (1985) present one list of seven strategies developed by Caplan (1964) and then describe a second list of seven strategies developed by McCubbin (1979). The two lists are not connected and only partially overlapping. The result is that the field does not have an integrated, coherent taxonomy or conceptual framework of coping strategies. McCubbin and Figley (1983) began the process of trying to integrate this literature, but they focused on correlates rather than coping strategies, and there has been considerable additional research since their attempt.

The methodology we used in trying to move toward a more coherent conceptual framework was first to identify original research where scholars developed ideas that are currently viewed as coping strategies. The next steps were to find rational or dictionary definitions of the terms that were used and to find the ways the concepts were operationalized. We then examined all of the strategies that had been identified and then grouped them into a meaningful and manageable conceptual framework.

The resulting conceptual framework has three different levels of abstraction. At the most specific level are the particular questions that are used to operationalize specific coping strategies. Examples of these are questions such as, Was a family honest, clear, and direct in expressing its affections? Were family members clear and direct in expressing commitment to one another? Some of these specific activities can be grouped together to form a set of coping strategies that are at an intermediate level of abstraction. For example, honest expression of affections and clear and direct expressions of commitment are two examples of an intermediate strategy that can be called "express feelings and emotions." The intermediate strategies also can be grouped together to form more abstract categories. For example, expressing feelings and affection is just one part of a more abstract strategy of trying to manage the emotional aspect of the family system.

Part of the challenge of reviewing the previous literature was determining whether the scholars were dealing with resources, correlates, or coping strategies. We found that scholars often used these three concepts interchangeably and in confusing ways, and we were left with the task of determining what they were attempting to do.

We began by looking at each original publication. This led to a long list of specific coping strategies. We then examined the comprehensive list and grouped the strategies in conceptually meaningful and useful ways; this led to the three-level conceptual framework. We believe, however, that the best way to communicate the results is to reverse the procedure and present the overall framework first. Then, after the framework is presented, it will be helpful to review the specific studies and sources of the ideas in the overall framework.

Table 7.1 summarizes the relatively general or abstract areas of the resulting conceptual framework. The table includes the 7 general areas where strategies have been identified and the 20 moderately abstract strategies that are within the general areas. Six of the seven general areas involve family aspects: cognition, emotion, relationships, communication, community, and spiritual life. The seventh general area refers to the individualistic process of trying to enhance individual development. As Boss (1987) has emphasized, managing family stress in families is often a combination of familial and individual processes.

Table 7.2 expands on the ideas in Table 7.1 by describing the specific strategies that occur in each of the 20 moderately abstract strategies. These specific strategies are the various ways that scholars have operationalized the more specific strategies described in the reviewed studies.

It is important to realize that this conceptual framework is not merely a list that was generated by our whims or as an ad hoc or speculative list of how families handle stress. An extensive body of literature provides the basis of the framework, which is well

Table 7.1 The Proposed Conceptual Framework of Coping Strategies

Highly Abstract Strategies	*Moderately Abstract Strategies*
Cognitive	1. Be accepting of the situation and others.
	2. Gain useful knowledge.
	3. Change how the situation is viewed or defined (reframe the situation).
Emotional	4. Express feelings and affection.
	5. Avoid or resolve negative feelings and disabling expressions of emotion.
	6. Be sensitive to other's emotional needs.
Relationships	7. Increase cohesion (togetherness).
	8. Increase adaptability.
	9. Develop increased trust.
	10. Increase cooperation.
	11. Increase tolerance of each other.
Communication	12. Be open and honest.
	13. Listen to each other.
	14. Be sensitive to nonverbal communication.
Community	15. Seek help and support from others.
	16. Fulfill expectations in organizations.
Spiritual	17. Be more involved in religious activities.
	18. Increase faith or seek help from God.
Individual Development	19. Develop autonomy, independence, and self-sufficiency.
	20. Keep active in hobbies.

grounded in empirical, conceptual, and theoretical literature. We believe it is important to document these intellectual foundations of the framework by reviewing how previous scholars have defined the various strategies and how they operationalized them. The relevant literature is reviewed in the next section of this chapter.

Table 7.2 Specific Strategies for Managing Family Stress

Cognitive Activities

Accept the situation and others.

1. Quickly accept and confront the situation (Caplan, 1964, p. 293; Kaplan, Smith, Grobstein, & Fischman, 1973, p. 63; McCubbin & Figley, 1983, p. 27).
2. Accept the differences in family members' responses to the situation (Gilbert, 1989, p. 620).
3. Accept limitations; do not try to do or be everything (Caplan, 1964, p. 296; Gilbert, 1989, p. 621).

Gain useful knowledge.

1. Find information and facts about the situation (Caplan, 1964, p. 294; McCubbin et al., 1976, p. 466).
2. Understand the essential nature of the situation (Kaplan et al., 1973, p. 63; McCubbin et al., 1976, p. 466).

Change how the situation is viewed or defined.

1. Separate the stress into manageable parts (Caplan, 1964, p. 293).
2. Do not have false hopes, but have faith in own ability to handle the situation (Caplan, 1964, p. 294).
3. Have an optimistic attitude of life, self, and others (Caplan, 1964, p. 294; Gilbert, 1989, pp. 621-622).
4. Do not blame others or become preoccupied with blaming; instead, be solution-oriented (Caplan, 1964, p. 295; Kaplan et al., 1973, p. 63; McCubbin & Figley, 1983, p. 27).
5. View it as a family-centered concern and not as an individual's problem (Kaplan et al., 1973, p. 64; McCubbin & Figley, 1983, p. 27).
6. Reframe the situation by defining the problem in a more positive way (Gilbert, 1989, p. 622).

Emotional Activities

Express feelings and affection.

1. Express positive and negative feelings and emotions openly (Caplan, 1964, p. 293; Kaplan et al., 1973, p. 64; Gilbert, 1989, p. 617; McCubbin et al., 1976, p. 466).
2. Be honest, clear, and direct in expressing affection (Gilbert, 1989, p. 618; Hill, 1949, pp. 128-130; McCubbin & Figley, 1983, p. 28).
3. Be clear and direct in expressing commitment to each other (McCubbin & Figley, 1983, p. 28).

Avoid or resolve disabling expressions of emotion.

1. Reduce anxiety by taking time to get away or relax when needed (Caplan, 1964, pp. 293-295; Gilbert, 1989, p. 619; McCubbin et al., 1976, p. 466).
2. Avoid or reduce disturbing emotional feelings by self-punishment, consuming alcohol, smoking, crying, and withdrawing (McCubbin et al., 1976, p. 466).
3. Be passive about the situation.

Table 7.2 Continued

Be aware of and sensitive to each other's emotional needs.

1. Be sensitive to each other's needs (Gilbert, 1989, pp. 620-621; McCubbin & Figley, 1983, p. 28).
2. Share feelings of the experience with each other to be more aware of each other's specific situation (Gilbert, 1989, p. 618).

Relationship Activities

Develop family cohesion and togetherness.

1. Do things together to develop and increase family integration (Angell, 1936, p. 14; Hill, 1949, pp. 130-131; McCubbin & Figley, 1983, p. 28).
2. Do things with children and maintain stability (Davis & Boss, 1980, p. 705; McCubbin et al., 1976, p. 466).

Maintain family adaptability and flexibility.

1. Be flexible and willing to change family roles, behaviors, and attitudes (Angell, 1936, p. 16; Gilbert, 1989, p. 620; Hill, 1949, p. 132; McCubbin & Figley, 1983, p. 28).

Cooperate as a family.

1. Be unified and committed to cooperating as a family (Gilbert, 1989, p. 619; Hill, 1949, pp. 128-130; Kaplan et al., 1973, p. 68; McCubbin & Figley, 1983, p. 27).
2. Offer family members mutual support and access to the family's collective coping experience (Kaplan et al., 1973, p. 64).

Build and improve trusting relationships with others.

1. Develop trusting relationships with others (Boss et al., 1979, p. 83; Davis & Boss, 1980, p. 706; McCubbin et al., 1976, p. 466).

Increase tolerance of one another.

1. Have more tolerance of family members (McCubbin & Figley, 1983, p. 28).

Communication Activities

Be open and honest.

1. Be open in your communication with other family members (Gilbert, 1989, p. 616; Hill, 1949, p. 141; Kaplan et al., 1973, p. 64; McCubbin & Figley, 1983, p. 28).
2. Be honest in your communication with others (Gilbert, 1989, p. 616; Kaplan et al., 1973, p. 64).
3. Exchange information with one another (Gilbert, 1989, p. 617; Kaplan et al., 1973, p. 64).
4. Talk to someone about the situation (Boss et al., 1979, p. 83).

Table 7.2 Continued

Listen to each other.

1.   Listen to other family members (Gilbert, 1989, p. 617).
2.   Be effective in the quantity and quality of your communication (Hill, 1949, p. 141; McCubbin & Figley, 1983, p. 28).

Be more sensitive to nonverbal communication.

1.   Be sensitive and aware of nonverbal communication (Gilbert, 1989, p. 618).

Community Activities

Seek help and support from others.

1.   Seek and accept help from relatives when needed (Caplan, 1964, p. 295; Davis & Boss, 1980, p. 706; McCubbin et al., 1976, p. 466; McCubbin & Figley, 1983, p. 29).
2.   Seek and accept help from community services when needed (Caplan, 1964, p. 295; McCubbin et al., 1976, p. 466; McCubbin & Figley, 1983, p. 29).

Fulfill expectations in organizations.

1.   Accept and live up to expectations of organizations to which the family belongs (Boss et al., 1979, p. 83).
2.   Remain part of your organizations or community (McCubbin et al., 1976, p. 466).

Spiritual Activities

Be more involved in religious activities.

1.   Be more involved in your religion and religious activities (Davis & Boss, 1980, p. 706; Gilbert, 1989, p. 620; McCubbin et al., 1976, p. 466).

Increase faith or seek help from God.

1.   Believe in God.

Individual Development Activities

Develop autonomy, independence, and self-sufficiency.

1.   Be involved in self-development; it allows for more independence and self-sufficiency (Boss et al., 1979, p. 83; Davis & Boss, 1980, p. 706; Hill, 1949, pp. 144, 147; McCubbin et al, 1976, p. 466).

Keep active in hobbies.

1.   Spend time on hobbies and activities with friends (Boss et al., 1979, p. 83).

SPECIFIC STRATEGIES AND SOURCES

Cognitive Activities

Accepting the Situation and Others

The first publication to mention this strategy was Caplan (1964). This research project was a series of observations and interviews of (a) families responding to premature birth, (b) women who give birth to abnormal babies, (c) families with one member stricken with tuberculosis, and (d) families suffering the death of a member. Caplan described this strategy as families needing to "confront the crisis . . . talk about and realize the danger, the pain, the trouble, the real element of the crisis . . . speak of unspoken fears, to grieve, and even to cry" (Caplan, 1964, p. 293).

The second study that mentioned acceptance of the situation was by Kaplan and associates (1973), who studied more than 50 families with children who were diagnosed and treated for leukemia. Each family was studied from the date the parents were informed of the diagnosis until 2 months after the child died to "identify adaptive and maladaptive coping responses by the family" (1973, p. 61). The researchers found that "as a prelude to making the necessary changes in living that the child requires, [the family] must accept the fact that [it has] a chronically and seriously ill child instead of a normal one" (1973, p. 63).

Another aspect of acceptance first mentioned in Caplan's study (1964) led to the suggestion that:

the person who acknowledges that he or she is in trouble, actively looks for help, and gratefully accepts it is on the way to a healthy solution of the crisis—not only because the help will help but also because the acceptance of it is a sign of healthy management of a difficult situation. (p. 295)

Gilbert's (1989) study on grief and coping of couples who had experienced a fetal or infant death also found that the acceptance of limitations was important (p. 621). While looking for "the ways in which they coped as individuals and as a couple" (1989, p. 608), Gilbert found that accepting differences in response to the situation was important to couples who remained stable or restabilized after a period of conflict. She discovered that "as couples became aware of the differences in their grief and the bases for these differences, they became more willing to allow their spouse to behave differently" (1989, p. 620).

McCubbin and Figley (1983) also listed this strategy as one of the 11 characteristics that distinguish "families who cope effectively with stress and either avoid or quickly recover from traumatic experiences" (1983, p. 27). They stated that "effective families are able to quickly accept that their family is being forced to struggle with a highly stressful event or series of events" (1983, p. 27).

Gaining Useful Knowledge

The first research project to mention this strategy was Caplan's (1964). Researchers described the importance of finding out the facts. They claimed that "it is not the truth, but our fantasies and dreams, that make cowards of us all. The great void of the unknown is infinitely more frightening than the known, however threatening that may be" (1964, p. 294).

McCubbin et al. (1976) also mentioned this strategy in their review of findings from a longitudinal study by Plag (1974). They studied families who experienced periods of husband and father absence because the men were reported missing in action or prisoners of war in the Vietnam conflict. The purpose of the study was to "determine the range of coping patterns the wives employed to adapt to the prolonged and indeterminate absence of a husband . . . and what they perceived to be helpful to them in overcoming the hardships encountered during the separation period" (1976, p. 462). The study reported that seeking resolution was important through "the wives' involvement in national [or] regional activities designed to seek a full accounting of their husband's status" (1976, p. 466).

Kaplan et al. (1973) identified the importance of families understanding the essential nature of the situation. In their study of families with children diagnosed with leukemia, the researchers found that "it is important for both parents to understand the essential nature of the illness as early as possible, preferably before the hospital that makes the initial diagnosis discharges the child" (1973, p. 63).

Changing the View or Definition of the Situation

Caplan (1964) was the first study to discuss this strategy. Caplan discovered four ways in which to view or define a situation. First, people were better off if they were able to "confront the crisis in manageable doses" because "no one is strong enough to look at an alarming and dangerous reality without some relief" (1964, p. 293).

Second, a person needs to have faith in his or her "ability to handle the crisis . . . not the meaningless comfort that the crisis will take care of itself" (1964, p. 294).

Third, a person should maintain an optimistic attitude about the situation, others, and life. This was mentioned first by Caplan (1964, p. 294) and more recently by Gilbert (1989), who found that "the positive view [couples] held of each other and their relationship" and also their "optimistic view of life," (pp. 621-622) were very important.

Fourth, a person should not blame others.

> Blaming is a way of avoiding the truth, of looking at an ephemeral might-have-been instead of looking at the problem at hand. Blaming may, indeed, make [a person] feel better momentarily, but it will make it harder . . . and less likely [for someone to] come out of the crisis strengthened. (p. 295)

Kaplan et al. (1973) also found in their study that couples were better off if they did not spend a lot of time blaming themselves or others. McCubbin and Figley (1983) also stated that "effective families get stuck only briefly on who is to blame for the current crisis or trauma and then move on to mobilize their resources to correct the situation together" (p. 27).

Another helpful way to define the situation was to see it as a family-centered concern and not as one individual's problem. This strategy was first mentioned in the research by Kaplan et al. (1973)

and was later included in the work of McCubbin and Figley (1983): "[E]ffective families quickly shift the focus of the problem or stressor away from one family member or set of family members and recognize it as a problem or challenge for the entire family" (1983, p. 27).

The final idea in this area is reframing the situation by defining the problem in a more positive way. Gilbert (1989) discovered that *reframing* was "a coping skill found to be extremely useful in the move toward a positive view of each other . . . changing the conceptual or emotional viewpoint of family members in order to change the meaning of behavior of family members without changing the actual facts" (1989, p. 622).

Emotional Activities

Expressing Feelings and Affection

Caplan (1964) first mentioned the idea that open expression of feelings was good for people experiencing stress. Gilbert (1989) reported that "to cry together and display deep emotions in each other's company was frequently seen as helpful" (p. 617).

Strong affectional ties between husband and wife are important, but so are ties between father and children, between mother and children, and among children themselves (Hill, 1949). Hill's study reaffirmed Angell's (1936) findings in this regard. Ties may be either verbal or nonverbal (McCubbin & Figley, 1983). Gilbert (1989) emphasized the physical aspect of the emotional ties: "[C]ouples who grieved together were physically available to each other when hugging, touching, or sometimes talking was needed" (p. 618). One final aspect of emotional ties as a coping strategy is that the feelings toward one another need to be expressed clearly and directly (McCubbin & Figley, 1983). Expressions of commitment to each other seem especially important.

Avoiding or Resolving Disabling Expressions of Emotion

Some coping behaviors can be interpreted as ways of minimizing disturbing emotional feelings. These are not considered effective ways to resolve concerns about the specific situation; in fact, the behaviors enable family members to avoid expressing emotion. Caplan (1964) first mentioned this strategy when he noted that people may need "respite" and sometimes even "assistance with the smallest everyday tasks" (pp. 293, 296). McCubbin et al. (1976) and Gilbert (1989) also mentioned the avoidance of feelings. For example, Gilbert's interviews with couples found that "spending time with each other, without any other obligations, was very helpful" (p. 619).

Anxiety-reducing coping behaviors include actions such as "self-punishment, consuming alcohol, smoking, crying, and withdrawing" McCubbin et al. (1976, p. 466). "Being passive" is another way to reduce anxiety.

Being Aware of and Sensitive to Each Other's Emotional Needs

McCubbin and Figley (1983) first presented this idea when they described effective families who tended "to recognize the need for conciliation, patience, and consideration" (p. 28). Some couples found that "by helping their spouse and focusing on meeting his or her needs they also benefited" (Gilbert, 1989, pp. 620-621). Gilbert also reported that sharing feelings of the experience together was very helpful for many couples, allowing them to be more aware of each other's specific situation.

Relationship Activities

Developing Family Cohesion and Togetherness

Family integration was one of the first ideas thought to be related to how well families adjusted to crisis. This was proposed by Angell (1936) after studying 50 families who encountered the Depression. He described *family integration* as "many bonds of coherence and unity running through family life, of which common interests, affection, and a sense of economic interdependence are perhaps the most prominent" (p. 15). Hill (1949) similarly described family integration as "the unifying phenomena seen in the sense of economic and emotional interdependence . . . strong affectional ties

... (and) a certain pride in the family traditions, and high participation as a family in joint activities" (pp. 130-131). McCubbin and Figley (1983) agree that high family cohesion or togetherness also involves "members who enjoy each other's company, miss each other when they are away, are proud to be part of the family, and speak with pride about each other" (p. 28).

Another aspect of cohesion involves doing things with children and trying to maintain stability. McCubbin et al. (1976), first described this part of integration: "the wives' commitment to maintaining stability in the family through investing in a home, through family activities and through investing in the children's future" (p. 466). Davis and Boss (1980) report similar findings while studying a rural sample of women who had experienced husband and father absence because of divorce.

Having Family Adaptability and Flexibility

The idea of family adaptability is the second oldest factor that was thought to be an important influence on how well families adjusted to crises. Angell (1936) first described family adaptability not as "the adaptability of the family members as individuals, but [as] the adaptability of the unit in meeting obstacles in its way" (p. 16). Hill (1949) expanded the definition:

[It is] the flexibility and willingness of family members to shift social roles if necessary, the acceptance of responsibility by all family members in performing family tasks, the presence of habits of collective discussion and control, and a repertoire of crisis meeting devices built out of previous successful experiences with trouble. Adaptability refers to the family's readiness to adjust as a unit to changed situations. (p. 132)

Other studies describe adaptability similarly (see Gilbert, 1989, p. 620; McCubbin & Figley, 1983, p. 28).

Cooperating as a Family

Hill (1949) first mentioned cooperation as it related to good marital adjustment. He described the importance of husband and wife being "in agreement on the chief issues of marriage" and settling their differences by "mutual give and take" (pp. 128-130). Additional studies encourage cooperation in the family during stressful times (Gilbert, 1989, p. 619; Kaplan et al., 1973, p. 68; McCubbin & Figley, 1983, p. 28). Each study explains the importance of having cooperation in the family and helping each other as much as needed.

Closely related to cooperation is an idea that Kaplan et al. (1973, p. 64) suggested: offering family members mutual support and access to the family's collective coping experience.

Building and Improving Trusting Relationships With Others

The first researchers to mention this strategy were McCubbin et al. (1976), who discussed the importance of developing "close relationships with others," and, specifically, relationships with others who are experiencing a similar situation (p. 466). Research done by Boss, McCubbin, and Lester (1979) as guided by Hill's (1949) study looked for the coping responses wives used and what they found to be helpful while their husbands were on naval ships for eight months. They also found "building and maintaining supportive relationships between family members and in the community" to be helpful (p. 240). Several other studies also agree with the idea of building close relationships with others (Boss et al., 1979, p. 83; Davis & Boss, 1980, p. 706).

Increasing Mutual Tolerance

The work by McCubbin and Figley suggest that "effective families' members tend to have even more tolerance for each other during a highly stressful time than in times of relative calm" (1983, p. 28).

Communication Activities

Being Open and Honest

Being open in communication as a strategy for dealing with stress was first discussed by Hill (1949), who stated that "crises of separation and reunion may be cushioned and even used to strengthen the relationship if the processes of communication are adequate and the avenues kept open" (p. 141). Many studies support the value of open communication (Gilbert, 1989, p. 616; Kaplan et al., 1973, p. 64; McCubbin & Figley, 1983, p. 28).

Honesty with others is another important aspect of communication (Kaplan et al., 1973). An atmosphere of honesty encourages family members to communicate because "frankness [allows] them to trust, respect, and love each other" (p. 64). Gilbert (1989) agreed that "open and honest communication has been seen as essential to recovery from loss. This allows partners to consider and validate each other's view of what has happened, is happening at present, and will happen in the future" (p. 616).

Exchanging information with each other was also presented as being important for families. Kaplan et al. (1973) reported that it is important for parents to inform the rest of the family about the true nature of an illness. Many if not all family members may need to be involved in a period of grief that follows an open and honest flow of information. This process enables some families to "face the inevitable outcome realistically and talk about it frankly" (p. 64).

Talking to someone about the situation was reported as being helpful by Boss et al. (1979), who studied the routine absence of corporate executive husbands and fathers to find the coping patterns used by their families. One result seen in their analysis was the importance of developing relationships with others and "talking to someone about how I feel" (p. 83).

Listening to Each Other

Gilbert (1989) was the first to really emphasize the importance of listening: "Frequently, couples spoke of a need to have their spouse simply listen to them and allow them to talk" (p. 617). An adequate and effective flow of communication is important (Hill, 1949; McCubbin & Figley, 1983), and listening increases the flow. McCubbin and Figley (1983) noted that effective families "tend to have few sanctions against when and what to talk about and, indeed, enjoy talking with one another about a wide range of topics" (p. 28).

Increasing Sensitivity to Nonverbal Communication

Another form of communication is nonverbal. Gilbert (1989) found that when couples found it difficult to express their thoughts and emotions to one another verbally, then nonverbal means of communicating were used instead of or in addition to the verbal means (p. 618).

Community Activities

Seeking Help and Support From Others

Seeking and accepting help from others, whether family, friends, or professional help in the community, is very helpful for families navigating stressful times. Several studies have identified the importance of seeking and accepting help from other family members (Caplan, 1964, p. 295; Davis & Boss, 1980, p. 706; McCubbin et al., 1976, p. 466; McCubbin & Figley, 1983, p. 29). Other studies support the importance of using community services when needed (Caplan, 1964, p. 295; McCubbin et al., 1976, p. 466; McCubbin & Figley, 1983, p. 29). Effective families are able to access their personal resources (both interpersonal and material) and nonfamily resources (either professional or nonprofessional) without difficulty and with little or no sense of embarrassment (McCubbin & Figley, 1983, p. 29).

Fulfilling Expectations in Organizations

McCubbin and Lester (1977) found that the degree to which families are able to accept and internalize expectations of organizations to which they belong and exhibit behaviors that reflect this acceptance affects how well they manage the stresses and demands of that organization. Boss et al. (1979) found similar ideas in their study of executives' wives. Related to this idea, is "remaining a part of the . . . community" (McCubbin et al., 1976, p. 64). Being able to fill outside expectations and remain a part of already existing networks is a strategy that helps families in stressful situations.

Spiritual Activities

Being More Involved in Spiritual and Religious Activities

McCubbin et al. (1976) found that many of their study subjects involved "themselves in religion and religious activities" as an effective way of dealing with stress (p. 466). Others have reported similar findings (Davis & Boss, 1980, p. 706; Gilbert, 1989, p. 620).

Increasing Faith or Seeking Help From God

A specific spiritual activity is to "believe in God." This belief and spiritual support in general may guide families in stressful situations because it contributes to maintaining the family unit and to individual self-esteem. It also serves as a reference point for social norms and expectations (McCubbin et al., 1976, p. 241).

Individual Development Activities

Developing Autonomy, Independence, and Self-Sufficiency

Many of the studies suggest that self-development is a very important part of dealing with stress. Hill's (1949) study was the first to address the issue and probably described these ideas best. Self-sufficiency and self-reliance of wives have a significant but curvilinear relationship to adjustment. "There is a provocative hypothesis to be tested in this finding that neither dependency nor extreme self-sufficiency makes for best adjustment in the face of dismemberment crises" (p. 144-147). Several other studies also support the importance of self-sufficiency and other individual traits (Boss et al., 1979, p. 83; Davis & Boss, 1981, p. 706; McCubbin et al., 1976, p. 466).

Keeping Active in Hobbies

Keeping active in hobbies was first mentioned by McCubbin and Lester (1977). Boss et al. (1979) also mention being involved in activities and concentrating on hobbies as a way of minimizing stress.

SUMMARY AND IMPLICATIONS

We hope that this conceptual framework will be useful to theorists, researchers, and practitioners interested in helping families who experience stress. Families often need assistance with understanding and working through family stress. It is important to remember that every family and each stressful situation is unique and that some of the described strategies may be more helpful for some families in certain situations. Having a large variety of possibilities is usually more helpful for families than having only one or two. Pearlin and Schooler (1978) found that "the sheer richness and variety of responses and resources that one can bring to bear in coping with life-strains may be more important in shielding one's self from emotional stress than the nature and content of any single coping element" (1978, pp. 14-15).

Several scholars also have identified coping strategies that tend to be harmful or disabling for families. McCubbin and Figley (1983, p. 29) cite violence and alcohol and drug use as ineffective methods of stress reduction. Although these ideas and others are also very important, they were few in number; we chose not to include them now in this framework of things that tend to be helpful.

Finally, it is important to remember that no coping strategy has been found to be a cure-all. Also, families can be involved inappropriately in any of the proposed beneficial activities mentioned if they are not aware of and respond to each family member's true needs.

EIGHT

When Are Coping Strategies
Helpful and Harmful?

McCubbin and Figley reviewed the previous research to identify coping strategies that are "universal and [which] transcend all types and categories of stressors" (McCubbin & Figley, 1983). There is, however, little research that has investigated whether the coping strategies they listed are helpful for a wide range of family stressors. A large proportion of the previous research dealt only with economic stressors. Several studies also focused on mental illness, and several have studied physical illness, but none of the earlier research dealt with several stressors in the same study.

We suspected at the beginning of our research that the universality of the helpfulness of McCubbin and Figley's list of strategies may be more complicated than earlier research has appreciated. For example, it may be that there are contextual factors related to whether some of the coping strategies are helpful. Also, some of the strategies may be helpful in coping with certain stressors but not others.

This chapter reports our efforts to learn more about these questions. Our first and main objective was to determine which coping strategies were effective for different types of stressors and which, if any, were helpful only in specific situations in our sample. Our second objective was to discover which strategies, if any, families find harmful. A third objective was to determine if some strategies were more helpful or harmful than others.

The issues we deal with in this chapter were influenced in several ways by the paradigmatic and theoretical orientations that guided the project. A systemic perspective assumes there are always contextual factors interacting with systems. Therefore, our concern was not whether there were contextual factors that made a difference, but how they made a difference.

Our presuppositions also led us to expect that there would be more diversity than previous research would lead us to believe. Therefore our research questions dealt with the proportion of families who found the various coping strategies helpful and harmful, not with which strategies are universally helpful or harmful.

METHODOLOGY

We included an 80-item questionnaire as part of the larger set of instruments. The questionnaire focused on how families used 80 coping strategies and how useful they found these strategies. The questionnaire was completed by 78 adults in 46 families. Each adult completed a separate questionnaire, and we then talked with them at length about their perceptions of the coping strategies they had tried and how useful they found them. This in-depth probing sought additional information about these issues and also about the recommendations that respondents had for other families facing similar situations.

Table 8.1 reproduces the first three items in our questionnaire to illustrate the way the questions were asked. Most of the 80 specific coping strategies were grouped into the 7 general strategy categories of Chapter 7: cognitive, communication, emotional, relationship, spiritual, community, and individual development. Some of these categories were so complex and included such different items that we subdivided them into subcategories. For example, the category of *relationship* strategies was divided into three subcategories: cohesion, adaptability, and a residual group called *other.* The entire list of categories can be seen in Table 8.2.

We used several different techniques to analyze the data. First, we determined how many of the respondents actually used each strategy. We were interested in this for two reasons: (a) we ultimately

Table 8.1 Questions Used to Determine Which Strategies Were Used and Their Helpfulness

When families encounter a "difficult" challenge, the family members do many things to try to manage their new situation. In some situations they try some things and in other situations they try to do different things. Read each of the following statements and then: (1) circle the number on the left side to show how much time, effort, or energy you put into each way of responding, and (2) circle the number on the right side to show the results of what you did. Leave blank any of the things that you did not try to do.

Amount of time, effort, or energy doing it

None	A little bit	Quite a bit	A great amount		Made things much worse	Did not make any difference		Made things much better
							Effects of what you did	
0	1	2	3	4	1. Tried to seek additional information.	-2	-1	0	+1	+2
0	1	2	3	4	2. Tried to have an optimistic attitude.	-2	-1	0	+1	+2
0	1	2	3	4	3. Separated the situation into manageable parts.	-2	-1	0	+1	+2

Table 8.2 Percentage of Respondents Finding Coping Strategies Helpful and Harmful

Category	Total	BK	DH	IN	MD	HC	TT
Cognitive Strategies	69/11*	60/14	83/3	56/26	85/2	73/9	84/1
Acceptance (4,5,6)	63/11	60/3	90/0	34/39	75/0	72/7	82/5
Knowledge (1,7)	73/8	61/13	76/0	75/6	86/9	71/11	100/0
Definition and Reframing (2,3,10,11,14,60)	70/11	59/20	82/6	59/26	95/0	76/9	70/0
Communication (15,16,17,18,19,20)	86/5	71/17	83/4	88/1	97/2	91/4	87/3
Emotional Strategies (21,22,23,24,26,27,28,29,30)	80/7	63/16	73/9	82/6	88/4	88/2	77/4
Relationship Strategies	78/4	67/6	86/5	75/3	94/1	81/1	75/0
Cohesion (70,71,75,77)	88/1	75/6	93/0	89/0	98/0	93/0	90/0
Adaptability (32,33,34,35,36,37,38,73,74)	74/6	63/8	87/7	72/2	93/2	75/2	69/0
Other (31,39,54)	73/3	63/3	79/5	64/9	91/0	76/0	67/0
Spiritual Strategies (43,44,45,46)	87/5	86/5	92/5	83/11	93/0	86/0	90/5
Community Strategies	72/7	47/26	60/11	68/7	84/2	39/5	94/0
External Support (48,49,50,51,52,53,55,56,68,69)	74/7	51/29	63/10	68/6	88/2	77/6	88/0
Fulfilling Expectations (76)	53/11	43/0	57/29	67/22	80/0	0/0	100/0
Individual Development (47)	82/4	38/0	88/0	88/6	100/0	91/0	75/25
Total Scores	75/7	61/10	80/6	72/11	90/2	75/3	83/4

Key: BK = Bankruptcy (*N* = 13)   MD = Muscular Dystrophy (*N* = 19)
DH = Displaced Homemaker (*N* = 8)   HC = Handicapped Child (*N* = 14)
IN = Infertility (*N* = 18)   TT = Troubled Teen (*N* = 6)

*69/11 means 69% found these strategies helpful and 11% found them harmful.

Total *N* = 78

151

wanted to know which strategies were helpful and harmful, and this could only be determined if people actually used the strategies; (b) we wanted to determine whether there were both extensively used and rarely used strategies. An average of 66% of the subjects used each strategy, and most of the strategies were used by more than 70% of the sample. Only a few dropped below 50%. Thus the strategies were fairly widely used. Appendix B at the end of the book reports the percentage of respondents who used each item.

We then devised two different ways to measure the helpfulness of the coping strategies. One was to determine the respective percentages of respondents who found each strategy helpful and harmful. The second method was to view the responses from "made things much worse" to "made things much better" as an interval scale ranging from 0 to 5. This allowed us to compute means for a helpfulness score. These percentages and means included only the items that were actually used by each family.

We initially thought it would be useful to analyze the means and percentages separately because we expected the two approaches to reveal different kinds of information. However, as we worked with the data we gradually realized that the two approaches revealed virtually identical information. We were unable to see any patterns or tendencies with the means that did not also appear with the percentage information. Also, as we discussed whether it was defensible to combine the information about whether a strategy made things worse or better, we gradually became uncomfortable with the interval-scale approach because it seemed to have two fairly different dimensions. One was the amount of helpfulness and the other was the amount of harmfulness. As a result, we present only the percentage data in this chapter.

We also analyzed each of the audio tapes of the interviews. We waited until we had the percentages in Table 8.2 and the mean helpfulness scores before we systematically listened to each tape because we wanted to use the quantitative information to help us have some ideas about what to listen for. Our goal in the analysis of the tapes was to see if the comments would add any additional insights to which we ought to pay attention. We wanted to find information such as which strategies were and were not used, which were helpful and harmful, whether there were gender patterns in the ways the respondents thought about and used the strategies, and whether there were any other patterns or ideas that did not appear in the quantitative information on the questionnaires. We also wanted to find comments that helped illustrate the differences and conclusions we had picked up from the quantitative data.

RESULTS

Table 8.2 summarizes the information about the helpfulness and harmfulness of the strategies in the conceptual framework of Chapter 7. The categories are listed on the left; the items that make up each category and subcategory of stressors are identified. The column of percentages at far left shows the average percentage of the total subjects who found the strategies to be helpful and harmful. The other six columns show the average percentage of subjects in each of the six different stressful situations who found each category of stressors helpful and harmful. The bottom row shows the total scores according to the six different stressors.

Several conclusions emerged from the column totals in Table 8.2. First, these coping strategies tended to be helpful most of the time. An overall average of 75% of the families found the strategies helpful, whereas more than 80% found many of the individual categories helpful. Thus the strategies that were included in the 80 items were relevant and useful to these families as they struggled with managing their stressful situations.

Second, these strategies are sometimes harmful. When looking at the overall situation, they were harmful 7% of the time. When we examined the specific areas and the different stressors, some of them are harmful fairly frequently. For example, the families coping with infertility found the acceptance strategies harmful 39% of the time.

Third, differences emerged in the bottom row between the six types of stressors: The strategies that were included in our list were the least helpful to the families who were coping with bankruptcy. On average, 61% of the families experiencing bankruptcy found these strategies helpful. The other stressors had considerably higher rates of helpfulness.

We were intrigued with the consistently lower usefulness rates of these strategies to the bankruptcy group. We found ourselves asking, what accounts for the difference in helpfulness? What is the difference between bankruptcy and these other stressors that would make these strategies less helpful for managing stress related to bankruptcy? We tried to determine why the strategies were generally less helpful to the families coping with bankruptcy by examining the quantitative data, listening to the audio tapes, and discussing our impressions from the interviews and observations. The idea we found the most useful is the distinction Foa (1971) has suggested between economic and interpersonal resources and goals. Foa's theory proposes that economic phenomena tend to be fairly universalistic and concrete, while interpersonal and emotional phenomena tend to be fairly particularistic and symbolic. He also theorized that the rules that govern economic processes are fundamentally different from the rules that govern interpersonal and emotional processes.

Bankruptcy undoubtedly involves a large number of interpersonal and emotional processes, but it may be that it is less of an interpersonal and emotional experience than stressors such as infertility, muscular dystrophy, and troubled teen. Also, the strategies that were included on our questionnaire tended to be relatively intrapersonal and interpersonal strategies as opposed to economic ones. Perhaps what those experiencing bankruptcy needed the most was economic resources and strategies rather than interpersonal ones. Put more bluntly, what they needed was money more than communication, acceptance, and redefinitions of their situation. Strategies such as acceptance and dealing with their feelings helped only a little. Thus, in a sense, we believe the data in this study provide a little bit of evidence in support of Foa's model.

Minor differences also were found between the other stressors in how helpful the families found the strategies included in this study. For example, the muscular dystrophy population found these strategies helpful more often than any other stressor group— 90%. Apparently, the stresses related to dystrophy are managed with these strategies more often than the other stressors in our project. The other four stressors were fairly similar; their overall usefulness ranged between 72% and 83%.

Several other differences in Table 8.2 also seem relevant. Some deal with differences between the types of coping strategies, and others deal with differences between the types of stressors. We decided to organize our discussion of these differences according to the differences in the categories of management strategies.

Cognitive Strategies

Cognitive strategies are the attempts that families make to change their intellectual processes. Examples are trying to accept a situation, trying to redefine or reframe what is happening, and getting new knowledge. One father illustrates these strategies: "The key thing is for people to accept the situation right off the bat and to try to deal with it instead of trying to hide the problem."

Cognitive strategies are one of seven general types. The left-hand column in Table 8.2 shows that seven types of coping strategies fell into three groups of helpfulness. Two categories—spiritual strategies and communication—were clearly most helpful, while cognitive and community strategies were clearly the least helpful. The most helpful strategies were helpful to some 85% of the families, and the least helpful strategies were helpful to approximately 67% of families. The cognitive strategies were helpful 69% of the time, indicating that they were the least helpful of all. Thus even though a majority of the families found the cognitive strategies helpful, they tended to be less helpful overall than all other strategies.

The finding that the cognitive strategies were the least helpful has an important implication for the family stress literature. The cognitive strategies have received a great deal of attention in the family stress literature and in the models developed by Lazarus, but our data suggest that these strategies are actually the least helpful of all strategies. This finding seems to suggest that we may have a cognitive bias in the earlier literature. We have overemphasized the importance of cognitive strategies and underemphasized the importance of some of the other strategies that are actually more helpful.

The subcategories with cognitive strategies were "trying to accept the situation," "getting more knowledge," and "redefining or reframing the situation." Some slight differences were seen among these three subcategories. Getting more knowledge and reframing were helpful some 70% of the time, and trying to accept the situation was useful 63% of the time.

The families we interviewed shared many insights about what was and was not helpful. For example, even though other strategies were more universally helpful, many families shared with us how and why they found the cognitive strategies helpful. According to one mother with a handicapped daughter, "What helped me the most is that I accepted it. I accepted that I have a child that's going to die or that is severely handicapped, and I didn't deny it. . . . And, I think acceptance was the major thing, just to accept that it's here and you have to do it."

A single mother who experienced difficulties related to having a troubled teenager shared the following about the helpfulness of acceptance and knowledge strategies:

"The thing that was the most helpful I think was getting help; accepting it as a problem and going to people who could help instead of keeping it a secret and trying to deal with it all myself. I think that's been the biggest thing, because I became willing early in the process to accept the way it was and accept whatever help I could get anywhere, learn anything new, just start over with the way I used to handle things and realize it didn't work. I was open to anything."

When we asked one of our respondents, a displaced homemaker, what advice she had for others, she said, "If they have never been out of the home before, they don't need to feel guilty or try to blame anyone else at all. I think they need to accept the situation, do what they can best do for their family. . . . The basic thing is not to feel guilt and blame and all that stuff because we have to leave the home."

Interesting differences also appeared by stressor type. The acceptance strategies were helpful to 90% of the displaced homemaker population and 82% of the troubled teen group, but only 34% of the infertility group. Even with the small Ns in our study, this difference was statistically significant. A one-way analysis of variance (ANOVA) was 3.66, significant at the .05 level. A Tukey's test showed that it was the uniqueness of the infertility group that was the key difference, but the bankruptcy group was also relatively low. The differences were less dramatic with the other cognitive strategies, although relatively fewer of the bankruptcy families found all of the cognitive strategies useful, and fewer of the infertility families found the defining and reframing strategies useful.

The difference between the acceptance scores in the displaced homemaker group and the infertility group is an interesting and perhaps meaningful finding. It suggests that there may be fundamental differences in these two types of stressors. We discussed these possibilities and have speculated about some of these differences. Why would acceptance be helpful for most displaced homemakers but harmful for most infertile couples? Perhaps it has to do with the implications of acceptance for these two stressor groups. For example, for displaced homemakers, accepting the situation may tend to move them toward solving some of the related difficulties (i.e., getting a job or attending school in preparation for a career and economic stability). However, for infertile couples, simply accepting the situation may not move them toward solutions in their situation. For example, in accepting that they cannot have children, an infertile couple may forego further efforts to conceive a child. In their acceptance of infertility, the couple may decide against further medical efforts or treatments that might have proven successful if pursued. Therefore, accepting the situation could be perceived as harmful. We will discuss the harmful strategies as a group later, but 39% of the infertility group found the strategy of acceptance as harmful. This suggests that acceptance strategies may be harmful more often than helpful in dealing with this particular stressor.

Merely accepting their situation was harmful to the couples who were coping with infertility, but gaining knowledge was helpful to most of them. One wife we interviewed who had been struggling with infertility during her 9 years of marriage expressed the following about the helpfulness of gaining knowledge about infertility:

"Since I was not raised with any kind of mention of infertility, in that people could not have children, it allowed me to have false expectations. I know that for ourselves, we talked about how our children would likely have fertility problems. If children are raised that way, or have that knowledge ahead of time, I think that the stress will be much less."

Another couple experiencing infertility also found the strategy of trying to get additional knowledge helpful:

"At first we tried to approach it from getting more knowledge on the situation. We took classes up at the U and I bought books. . . . That helped to an extent, at least you felt like you knew what you were talking about. . . . I think that helped us get a little more in control at first."

These comments by people struggling with infertility support the finding that knowledge strategies are more helpful than acceptance strategies for managing this particular stressor.

The attempts to redefine or reframe the situation were more helpful to the families coping with dystrophy than any other group:

"It helped us to change how we thought about the illness. As long as we thought about what our son couldn't do and how tragic it was, we really struggled. Later, as we realized there are a lot of blessings in the situation it was helpful. We were learning how to be patient. Also many people were inspired by the way Brent handled his situation, and our family might not be as close as we are if we didn't have his problem. And, we've wondered if it hasn't been good for him in some ways. He's developed some beautiful traits like determination, sensitivity, and optimism and tolerance."

Another way of examining the data that we found useful was to look at the 80 items separately for additional insights. We were particularly interested in seeing which specific items were the most useful. Table 8.3 shows the rank order of the 16 most helpful items. None dealt with cognitive strategies.

It seems apparent from our respondents' comments that although cognitive strategies are helpful, they are coping strategies only, not cures. They seem to help in dealing with the problems and perhaps relieve some stress, but many other strategies also are needed, and more needs to be done than merely accepting, gaining knowledge, and redefining or reframing a situation.

Table 8.3 Rank Order of the Most Helpful Items

Rank		Item	Percentage Finding Item Helpful
1	37	Changed basic values as a result of the situation.	96
2	20	Tried to be understanding of each other.	93
3	55	Tried to talk with others in similar situation.	93
4	27	Tried to be more sensitive to each other's emotional needs.	92
5	45	Tried to have more faith in God.	92
6	71	Tried to focus on common goals and values.	91
7	17	Tried to listen to each other more.	91
8	44	Tried to get help through prayer or spiritual assistance.	90
9	39	Tried to cooperate more as a family.	89
10	36	Changed basic philosophy of life as a result of situation.	88
11	75	Tried to increase family togetherness (integration).	87
12	77	Tried to do more things as a family.	87
13	49	Tried to get help or encouragement from community organizations.	87
14	70	Tried to share the situation or experience as a family.	86
15	22	Tried to express affection more.	86
16	24	Tried to be honest, clear, and direct in expressing affection.	86

Communication Strategies

Overall, the communication strategies were quite helpful: 86% of those who used them found them valuable. This is therefore one of the two most helpful categories. Several respondents reported that communicating and listening were among their most helpful strategies. According to one displaced homemaker, "[I] have really found that after some tragedies that have happened that I have got to put our family first, and really sit and listen and communicate, and put all of the family problems number one and then all of the other problems will balance out and work out."

A couple dealing with infertility commented about the communication strategies. "Victor helped me the most. He listened to me. We've supported each other, and we don't blame. We talk to each other but don't point the finger. It's nobody's fault. It just happened."

A couple going through bankruptcy also found communication to be helpful. "[S]haring all of this stuff with the family and letting the kids see what was going on and letting them share in the disappointments too, just really helped them grow too. . . . If they don't learn when they're young it's going to be a lot harder when they get older. And they may not be able to deal with it."

Another couple going through infertility shared the following information when asked what was helpful and what advice or help they would offer others going through infertility.

> WIFE: Understanding that we weren't alone in the situation. Getting the problem out in the open really helped a lot. Learning to express our needs to each other was really important.
> HUSBAND: Learning to listen to what she's trying to express.

A couple who had gone through years of dealing with infertility and had finally become pregnant gave the following answer when asked what three things helped them most in dealing with their infertility struggles. "Communication and support would be one category and then be able to have a sense of humor and also be able to put things in perspective. I think humor allows you sometimes to put things in perspective. . . . Third, I'd say take an active role in solving your problem as much as possible."

The data indicate minor differences between the different kinds of stress. The communication strategies were the most helpful to the families with dystrophy (97%) and the least helpful to the families with bankruptcy (71%). These differences were not statistically significant because of the small Ns, but they are consistent with findings about most other stressors. That differences exist even in a small population is striking and provides support for the idea that we should look for patterns in complex family processes rather than one-to-one causal laws. Statistical tests for significance in these communication and other strategies provide a beginning basis for looking for broad, general patterns.

Six of the 80 items in the questionnaire dealt with communication strategies, and 2 of these items were among the top 16 in Table 8.3: item 17 (Tried to listen to each other more), with 91% finding it helpful, and item 20 (Tried to be understanding of each other), with 93% finding it helpful. This suggests that within the area of communication, these two strategies were the most helpful in managing family stress. The comments of a woman who had been displaced from her home illustrate this point. "The thing now is to deal with it face to face, head on, but understand that the person doesn't need to be dealt with in a negative way. They don't need to know their downfalls. They don't need to know what they did wrong. They know that. They're there. They're the one that's hurt. They need encouragement. They need support. They need more love. A listening ear. Just let them talk it out. Let the person talk it out. They are at a point where you can give your input, where you can tell how you feel, but there is a limit to that. The person doesn't need to have someone keep nagging and nagging. 'You did this, and . . .' I don't need that. I know what I've done. I know the consequences. I need help now. I need positive input. I need positive help that is going to help me to find the situation that is best to solve the problem. Too many times families are too critical and too judgmental."

This woman seems to be saying that listening and understanding are indeed a big part of what she needs from others to help her through the difficult stresses she is dealing with in displacement.

Emotional Strategies

We were curious to see how helpful these strategies were because they are given considerable emphasis in family stress literature. For example, McCubbin and Dahl (1985) and Caplan (1964) spend more time talking about the value of dealing effectively with emotional processes than any other management strategy. One family illustrates how it was useful to deal deliberately with its emotions: "We would go along fine for a while, and then something would come up that would be upsetting. Like . . . he would be teased by the kids at school. He would not be able to do something he could before. He would have to go into braces. A dance would come up at school, and we'd realize he's not included. Or, one of us would just get discouraged. We'd cry on each other's shoulders. We'd talk, and try to get our feelings out so they wouldn't last and make things worse. We tried really hard to 'be there' for each other when we needed it."

A large number of the families commented on how they benefited from cultivating their feelings of love. For example, "I think if you just continue to talk with your family and . . . don't have any blame for it but just love your family and try to stay together as a family, it's pretty simple.

"I thought on more than one occasion in the midst of wondering where we were headed with all of this that as long as we keep trying and doing the best we could and be understanding and loving and all the things that we were trying to do that it would be fine and it wouldn't take forever to do it. When you have a reassurance like that it's much easier."

In our sample, 80% of the respondents found these strategies helpful (which indicates that emotional strategies are very helpful), although not the most helpful. They ranked fourth in helpfulness among the seven categories.

Table 8.2 indicates only minor differences with regard to emotional strategies between the six stressor situations. Again, the families with bankruptcy found these strategies the least helpful, and the families with dystrophy and a handicapped child found them most helpful. The slight differences between the stressors is almost exactly the same pattern as with the cognitive and communication strategies. The only exception to this pattern with emotional strategies is that the percentage of families with a handicapped child is as high as the families with dystrophy.

Nine of the 80 items dealt with emotional strategies, and 3 were among the top 16 in Table 8.3. The top emotional strategies were items 27 (Tried to be more sensitive to each other's emotional needs—92%), 22 (Tried to express affection more—86%), and 24

(Tried to be honest, clear, and direct with expression of affections—86%). The following comment illustrates how being open about feelings is helpful.

"To learn how to not become so withdrawn from the situation, not letting anyone know what you're feeling—and I know that I found that the more open I am and the more I tell people who question us—if I'm just open and say, 'If you only knew what we're trying to do to have children,' then the stress is taken off of me. . . . It takes a long time to get from something that you're ashamed of and the judgment that people are putting on you to get to be able to be open with people and say, 'Well this is what's happening with me' and people start to realize that they're making judgments and maybe they shouldn't be."

Relationship Strategies

The strategies that dealt with relationships were helpful 78% of the time. Even though 78% is quite high, this is only the fifth most helpful category. These strategies are in the middle group of three strategies that were helpful 78%, 80% and 82% of the time.

Of the 80 items in the questionnaire, 16 dealt with relationship-managing strategies. This allowed us to differentiate three different subcategories: cohesion, adaptability, and a residual group we called *other.* The differences among these three subcategories turned out to be more important than we expected.

Cohesion was most helpful 88% of the time, and this was the highest average of all categories and subcategories. The other two subcategories were helpful less often, approximately 74% of the time. Because the cohesion strategies dealt with helping family members become closer, remain close, and be supportive, this suggests that these ways of relating to others during stress are more likely to be helpful than trying to be adaptable or improving other aspects of relationships.

One of our respondents, a father, shared how his experience with family cohesion helped him through some of the family's tough times. He stated the following about his wife. "She has a tremendous family, and I know the reason that she is that way,

because her family is that way. They are the most upbeat, optimistic people even in the midst of problems and troubles, and even
when they're down they'll still have a big party for somebody.
That's the way they are. That's the way she is. Thank God for Sherrie
and her family. Otherwise, I'd lead a very dull life."

Another example of how cohesion strategies helped is from the
family with a displaced homemaker. She shared her beliefs about
the need for her extended family's cooperation and help in dealing
with their stress. "To me a true family is a family that can cope.
That can help one another through a difficult time, no matter how
severe it might be. That's love. That's a real family. It takes a strong
family to deal with it the right way."

Another family, this one struggling with a troubled teenager,
also found family cooperation very helpful. "You know just the
fact [of] her going through all this pulled people together too,
where we kinda had a common cause. Everybody would go to the
hospital to visit her. Everybody would make a big deal when she
came home for visits. It was a real fun thing for everybody. There
was less fighting. The ones who really were probably most angry
and fighting the most were happy when she came home, and so it
really did lessen the contention. And then she's very supportive of
the family and things that we try to do now."

The two system characteristics of adaptability and cohesion
have been grouped together in research ever since Angell's (1936)
study of stress in the 1930s. The linking of these two that has received the most attention is Olson's circumplex model (1976). Most
of the research that has linked these two together has not had data
that compared their relative value; our data, however, provide a
little comparative information. Both characteristics are helpful, but
apparently strategies that deal with cohesion are helpful more of
the time than strategies that deal with adaptability. Adaptability
strategies are helpful approximately 75% of the time, but cohesion
strategies are helpful 90% of the time.

The stressor-specific differences are about the same with relationship strategies as with the others. They are least useful to families coping with bankruptcy and most helpful to families coping
with dystrophy. One slight difference is that adaptability is less

helpful in coping with infertility and troubled teens. These differences have some intuitive sensibility. Tenacity and determination may be more helpful than adaptability in dealing with infertility, and considerable literature suggests that when coping with teenage behavior problems, families are often better helped by becoming more firm and "tough" (Neff, 1982).

The families with displaced homemakers found cohesion strategies to be the most helpful of all categories. These strategies were helpful 93% of the time. One displaced homemaker shared some of the things that she felt helped her the most, one of which dealt with cohesion. "Number one, my faith in the Lord. Two, having a focus on a career, rather than just a job, and the third—I would say trying to look at the future as a more positive thing and getting closer to the children."

Another indicator that the relationship strategies are highly useful is that 7 relationship items are in the top 16 items in Table 8.3. Of interest is that all 4 of the cohesion items were in the top 16.

Spiritual Strategies

The strategies that dealt with the spiritual part of life were some of the most helpful of all. The difference between the 87% for this category and the 86% for communication strategies is negligible, so the best conclusion is that spiritual and communication strategies were the most helpful.

The helpfulness of these strategies is illustrated by the families' comments. For example, a divorced woman with a handicapped child reported, "What helps me is what I believe as far as religion and believing that there's an afterlife and that she will have a body and it will be whole and that someday I hope I can see her again. I know through talking with parents who don't believe that, that's where their hardship comes in. You have to believe that there is something beyond now and that it's all for the good. I believe that this happened to me and my family to make us learn and grow and to make us love each other more. There was something that we had to live through, and we will. And we'll grow from it. So I think it was to our advantage. I feel sorry for the people who don't get to experience this, because I only see the good—only good comes out of it."

A couple with a muscular dystrophic child summarized the help from the spiritual part of their life: "The most important thing is that you have a spiritual belief and you do believe that there is something after and that you will be together as a family after a while, and this is just a temporary thing, and it's something you have to overcome."

Another mother with a handicapped child shared, "What helped me was that I had a good foundation as far as religion. Prayer pulled me through."

One interesting finding is that the spiritual strategies were clearly the most helpful to the families coping with bankruptcy. The 86% who found spiritual strategies helpful is 11% higher than the next most useful strategies for the families coping with financial difficulties. Unlike the other categories, the bankruptcy group found these strategies to be helpful nearly as often as the other stressor groups. In fact, their percentage is higher than the infertility group in this category, who had the lowest score of 83%. For some reason the bankruptcy group found these strategies helpful much more often than any other strategies we identified.

One family coping with bankruptcy helps us understand why they found these strategies helpful: "When the chips are down for me, boy, I'm on my knees a lot. . . . In those times of stress . . . it was the prayer and faith that knowing that if I was faithful, that the Lord would bless me through this time. . . . That for me was a big thing through it all."

Two of the spiritual strategies were among the top 16 in Table 8.3: "Tried to get help through prayer or spiritual assistance" and "Tried to have more faith in God."

Community Strategies

The strategies that deal with the ways families interact with the larger community are diverse. The result is that the overall percentage of 72% for this group is less informing than looking at the percentages for the subcategories of seeking support and trying to fulfill expectations.

Seeking community support is a strategy that has been included in the literature since the beginnings of scholarly inquiry about family stress. Therefore, we expected it to be a very helpful set of strategies. Our data indicate that it is helpful to a majority but may not be as universally helpful as scholars have assumed. Only 51%, approximately half, of the families coping with infertility found their attempts to get community support helpful. At the other extreme, 88% of the families coping with troubled teens and dystrophy found community support helpful.

Even though the overall percentage is lower than most other categories of strategies, many respondents, especially in the infertility group, suggested that support groups, a form of external support, were very helpful. For example, one couple revealed the following in discussing their struggle with infertility.

WIFE: Seeking help from outside, from other professional people—RESOLVE for instance, from other people that have the same type of problem was what helped me a lot.

HUSBAND: We got more information to find out what are our real options at this point. Having the help from outside people, and a lot of support from the people in that profession.

Another way of summarizing the value of external support is from a couple that had gone through bankruptcy. "I think two of the best things you can do are, number one, confide in your spouse and help them as much as you can, and number two, find out from someone who has been there so that they can help relieve the stress and say, 'Hey, you're going to live through this.' "

Our analysis of the differences between the stressors suggests that, with one exception, the helpfulness of community support is related to the availability of community agencies that focus on the particular type of stress. The sample was all gathered from the metropolitan area within 50 miles of Salt Lake City, Utah. We do not know of any community organizations that focus on bankruptcy. There is some community attention geared toward helping displaced homemakers. The local community college offers courses through a program funded by the state. At the other extreme, 88% of the families coping with dystrophy and troubled teens found community resources helpful. The University of Utah Medical School has a muscle clinic, and the state has an active chapter of the Muscular Dystrophy Association; these two agencies provide considerable assistance to these families. Also, several hospitals and schools in the community specialize in helping families deal with teenage behavior problems. This suggests that these organizations are relatively effective and that no comparable associations exist for many of the other stressors.

The exception to the general conclusion is with families coping with infertility. The medical school has a unit that focuses on infertility, and there is the support group RESOLVE. Yet a smaller percentage of the families found community resources helpful. We suspect that the smaller percentage of families finding this support helpful is not because of the absence of help, but rather because of the limited ability of the agencies to help the families conceive and the higher expectations many of the families initially have when they try to get help.

Another finding that emerged from the interviews and the questionnaire was that a large number of families found it helpful to join support groups. For example, a divorced woman who had three handicapped children: "For sure, talk to people that have gone through it. For sure. They can really relate to what you're going through. And that's good if they can get into any kind of support group. I would encourage that."

Several couples coping with infertility found their participation in RESOLVE valuable. "Through RESOLVE we've been able to talk to other couples and get other ideas, learn more about procedures that are available in other parts of the country. . . . Try and focus on the more positive, the success stories. Talk to people that have had successes. If all you hear is gloom and doom all the time, it's hard to keep your feelings up and be optimistic about things. . . . I think that helped to kind of keep me going and almost convince me that I was not going to accept the fact that I could not have a child."

Another couple had the following comments.

WIFE: We joined RESOLVE. When we first started going through this we did not want to talk about it to anyone—period. We just shut it off. And I had to talk to somebody. And we didn't tell our family or tell any of our friends what we were doing, and I felt like I was going to explode—so I joined RESOLVE. There were people there who were going through the exact same thing as us. When you find that, you realize that you're not going crazy and there's other people in your situation. I got really active in it.

HUSBAND: Anybody involved in a stress situation should get involved with a support group. At first you think, "Well, it's not really what I want to do." But you find out after you're into it that you find common ground with somebody that just makes moving through and getting to a resolution a lot faster. Talking about it helps you get stress relief.

WIFE: I think that there's satisfaction of being able to help others. Seeing that maybe you were in their situation maybe a year ago and you're able to help them out and get them to where you're at. There's a lot of satisfaction in that.

Even though most of the respondents recommended support groups for those who are struggling, not all support groups are for everyone. This was made clear by the following comment from a mother with a child with muscular dystrophy: "I sat in a parent support group. Everyone was so down. They cried, and they tried to compare whose kid had it worse. So from that point on we never wanted to have anything to do with a support group because it took us down."

The other subcategory, being able to fulfill expectations outside the home, is unique. We included it because it appeared in the research on military families coping with missing family members, but we only included one item, which limits the generalizations that can be made about this as a category of strategies. However, keeping this caution in mind, there were interesting results.

This strategy was the least helpful overall and the most diverse. The percentage of families finding this strategy helpful ranged from 0% to 100%, with an average of 53%. The troubled teen group had the highest score, with 100% of respondents finding this strategy helpful. We suspect this may be related to the nature of this stressor. Teenagers are all involved with schools; when teens get into trouble, the school is invariably involved. Apparently, focusing on fulfilling expectations is a helpful strategy for these families. At the other extreme, when a young child is severely handicapped, focusing on fulfilling expectations of groups outside the family is not helpful. This is a unique finding. In every other category the handicapped children group had at least 70% of respondents finding the strategies helpful. This finding points out the differentiation that exists between kinds of stressors and coping strategies. Not all types of family stress are alleviated by using the same strategy. The fact that we had a total of 14 respondents suggests that this may be a replicable finding. If it had occurred with one of the groups with only 6 to 8 respondents, then it would be more suspect.

In sum, 11 of the 80 items in the questionnaire dealt with community strategies. Two were in the top 16 in the percentage of respondents who found them useful: items 49 (Tried to get help or encouragement from organizations in the community—87%) and 55 (Tried to talk with others who have a similar situation—93%). Thus it appears that seeking external support is helpful to most families in managing stressful life circumstances. In addition to the more formal support groups, many of the families also found less formal interaction with others who were in similar situations helpful. Consider, for example, the following observations of a woman with a muscular dystrophic child.

> WIFE: And I think it helps to talk with people who have children with the same disease. That really helps. You know, if you talk with our neighbors—like if I talk with them—they don't understand because they don't know what the situation is like. But if you talk with someone who has the same kind of situation, they understand where you're coming from when you complain because he's beating into the walls, you know, or doing something silly like that. Because it bugs ya. The wheelchair, as you can see, just beats the heck out of your house. But they don't understand because they don't have that kind of situation. So it really helps to talk to somebody, I think, with the same situation.

Individual Development

This strategy is conceptually unique, but we only included one item about it. Thus we were not sure whether it was defensible to refer to it as a category of strategies. In retrospect, we wish we had included more items about individual development. We considered not including this category, but it has been talked about in the literature and is conceptually unique. However, in trying to compare it to the other categories, we need to remember that only one item samples this category of strategies.

This strategy was helpful to a large majority of those who used it in a variety of stressful situations. The average percentage who found it helpful was 82%, third in overall helpfulness of the seven stressors. The following comment by a woman coping with being a displaced homemaker illustrates how this strategy helped. "I've had individual therapy and group therapy, and I think you need both of them. I think going to college helped me a lot, because I was doing something for me that was important to me. It was a goal, and it was the only area I felt good about. I knew that I was bright, and I knew that I could do that, so I took something that I was successful in and reached a goal, and I think that helped me have the strength to do other things."

This strategy also had variation in helpfulness across the stressors. The pattern was essentially the same as with the other categories. The fewest families finding this strategy helpful were those coping with bankruptcy (38%); the stressor in which the most families found this strategy helpful was dystrophy (100%). These differences, like the cognitive strategies, were substantial enough that even with our small totals they were statistically significant. The F-ratio with a one-way ANOVA was 2.55, significant at the .03 level. Again, this difference is largely because the bankruptcy group was so different from the others.

Results From Harmful Strategies

The notion that some coping strategies are actually harmful has not been extensively discussed or researched. McCubbin and Dahl

(1985) suggested that some coping strategies are ineffective for solving some family problems and that some strategies may even become a source of stress by making some problems worse.

We were interested in learning more about what types of strategies tend to be harmful and whether there were stressor specific differences in how much they are harmful. We therefore included in our questionnaire several items that described strategies that McCubbin and Dahl suggested tend to be negative or harmful activities. Strategies were included in the following categories: communication, cognition, emotion, and relationship. The harmful strategies have to do with poor communication, not accepting the situation, denying the situation, not expressing or hiding emotions, and acting in ways that break down relationships and destroy trust.

Ten items dealt with harmful strategies in our list of 80 strategies. These strategies and the percentage of people who found them helpful and harmful are shown in Table 8.4. We included the percentage of people who found these strategies helpful and compared them with the percentage that found them harmful because in some situations there are interesting patterns.

We were not surprised when the data revealed that the respondents found these strategies harmful most of the time. We were, however, surprised to learn that, even though they found them harmful 60% of the time, they found these harmful strategies *helpful* 24% of the time. This reinforces the point that many scholars have been arguing for in recent years: The family realm is more complicated, variable, and complex than is generally recognized (Beutler et al., 1989; Constantine, 1986; Walker, 1985). More specifically, the conclusion that emerges from these data is that what works in some situations does not work in others, and processes that are often or usually disruptive are helpful and facilitating in some situations.

The data about these harmful strategies seem to be most meaningful when we look at them individually in the different stressful situations. With regard to bankruptcy, trying to keep feelings inside was harmful more often than any other strategy. Also, wishing and daydreaming were not very helpful or harmful.

Table 8.4 Percentage Finding the "Harmful" Strategies Helpful or Harmful

Category	Total	BK	DH	IN	MD	HC	TT
Acceptance							
8. Denied, avoided, or ran away from problem.	*26-53	32-41	9-58	15-67	36-43	28-46	15-75
	30-70	50-50	0-80	17-83	63-38	20-60	0-100
62. Acted as if nothing had happened.	33-60	40-60	0-100	18-82	44-56	18-79	0-100
64. Wished or daydreamed that situation would end or somehow be over.	12-26	10-20	14-29	7-27	22-22	17-25	0-100
65. Sought to forget entire matter.	22-50	14-29	33-33	20-70	0-50	33-17	50-50
72. Waited for problem to go away.	33-59	44-44	0-50	13-75	50-50	50-50	25-25
Communication							
63. Sought to keep others from knowing how bad the situation was.	14-70	42-58	25-75	0-87	40-50	33-56	25-75
Emotions							
23. Expressed affection less.	24-71	35-65	0-58	14-86	40-60	9-57	75-0
61. Kept feelings inside.	33-67	50-50	0-33	20-80	50-50	0-50	100-0
	14-75	20-80	0-83	8-92	30-70	18-64	50-0
Relationships							
13. Became more critical of others.	22-63	27-59	10-55	10-70	33-58	50-9	0-100
78. Took out feelings on others	19-51	14-57	0-50	7-64	40-40	50-17	0-100
	25-75	40-60	20-60	13-75	25-75	50-0	0-100
Totals	24-60	32-51	10-59	12-74	36-50	29-42	25-65

Key: BK = Bankruptcy (*N* = 13)   HC = Handicapped Child (*N* = 14)
MD = Muscular Dystrophy (*N* = 19)   IN = Infertility (*N* = 18)
DH = Displaced Homemaker (*N* = 8)   TT = Troubled Teen (*N* = 6)

*26-53 means 26% of respondents found these strategies helpful and 53% found them harmful.

173

Several interesting patterns appeared with the group coping with displaced homemaker status. Denial seems to be particularly disruptive for this situation. If the groups tried to go on as if nothing had happened, this was harmful all of the time. Denial, probably selectively used, seems to help almost half the time with bankruptcy and dystrophy, but it was never helpful with displaced homemakers and troubled teens. Also, with both displaced homemakers and troubled teens, 6 of the 10 items were never helpful.

With regard to infertility, concealing it from others was the only strategy that was never helpful, but daydreaming and being critical of others were almost never helpful. Denial and concealing it from others apparently are particularly harmful with this type of stressor. Also, trying to express affection seems to be much more disruptive when families are coping with infertility than with the other stressful situations.

Dystrophy is unique in several interesting ways. Denial was helpful 63% of the time, and merely waiting for the problem to go away was helpful half the time. The overall totals for this situation indicate that these harmful strategies tend to be helpful in this particular situation more than the other situations. We are not sure why this is so, but strategies such as concealing, being critical, expressing affection less often, and trying to go on as if nothing has happened are often helpful. The strategy that was harmful most frequently was trying to keep feelings inside.

When families are coping with a handicapped child, they never found it helpful to express less affection, and trying to go on as if nothing had happened was harmful the most. It may not be noble, but trying to take it out on others was helpful half of the time. Apparently, there is something about this situation and bankruptcy that leads to a little vindictiveness—which seems to be helpful.

The troubled teens group had the most dramatic differences and extreme patterns. The findings need to be tempered by the small number (6) we studied, but the patterns are dramatic. Denial and disrupting relationships were always harmful. Yet, at the other extreme, expressing less affection was always helpful rather than harmful. Apparently, when families are coping with difficulties with their teens, they find the strategy of greater emotional distance or withholding affection helpful. This is, of course, quite different from the other stressful situations. These families also found that keeping their feelings inside helped half the time.

It appears that McCubbin and Dahl (1985) were generally right in reference to harmful strategies: Several strategies usually make problems worse for families when they are trying to manage stress. However, it is important also to have discovered that the strategies that tend usually to be harmful are actually helpful in some situations. Also, what is harmful and helpful depends, at least partially, on the nature of the stressful situation. We were surprised at how often the harmful strategies were helpful, and these findings set the stage for additional research to help us better understand the conditions under which these strategies tend to be helpful and harmful.

THE ROLE OF GENDER

We also wanted to determine any meaningful differences between men and women. We computed the response means on an interval scale ranging from 0 to 5. A zero indicated that using of the strategy made things much worse, and a 5 indicated that the strategy made things much better.

Men and women did not differ on 70 of the 80 strategies. However, they did show a significant difference with 10 strategies. Table 8.5 lists those exhibiting gender differences.

Two trends were evident in the data. First, women appear to use a wider range of coping strategies than men. The strategies they found more helpful included one or more strategies from five of the categories. Again, the spiritual strategy ranked near the top and the cognitive strategy near the bottom. In general, women tend to reach out to others, share concerns with friends and relatives, be more involved in religious activities, spend more time on themselves or hobbies, analyze situations, try to manage them in small parts, and express feelings openly. Missing from this group of strategies are any mention of coping strategies from the communication and

Table 8.5 Differences Between Men and Women

Strategy	F Value	Women	Men	Category
More Useful for Women				
53. Shared concerns or difficulties with friends.	.001	4.39	3.80	Community
46. Sought more involvement in religion.	.023	3.66	2.00	Spiritual
52. Shared concerns or difficulties with relatives.	.012	4.10	3.62	Community
47. Tried to spend time on self-development or hobbies	.016	4.18	3.38	Individual Development
3. Separated the situation into manageable parts.	.029	4.05	3.59	Cognitive
69. Sought and accepted encouragement from friends.	.041	4.15	3.68	Community
21. Openly expressed positive and negative feelings and emotions.	.058	4.20	3.75	Emotional
More Useful for Men				
41. Used alcohol more.	.023	2.00	3.66	Other
61. Kept feelings inside.	.024	1.79	2.40	Harmful
63. Kept others from knowing how bad things were.	.051	2.00	2.50	Harmful

$p < .05$.

relationship categories. With our limited data we are only able to speculate why this is so. Men and women apparently find coping strategies in these two categories equally valuable.

Second, differences between men and women show that men tend to use more of the harmful types of strategies that indicate withdrawal, while women seek strategies that help them reach out to others. Men differed in their use of alcohol, trying to keep feelings inside, and trying to keep others from knowing how bad things were.

SUMMARY

McCubbin and Figley (1983) suggested they had identified a list of universal strategies that transcended every type and category of stressor. Our data provide several important refinements to this idea. Our data underscore a generalization that has been emphasized in considerable scholarship in the last decade such as Walker's (1985) essay about stress and Constantine's (1986) theory and data. The generalization is that there is vast variation in the family realm. Families differ considerably in how they function and in what helps them accomplish their goals. Even the best and most constructive strategies are not universally helpful, and strategies that are usually harmful are helpful in some situations. Our data, from a relatively small, homogeneous sample underscore the variation and yet indicate the possibility of finding general patterns that can be widely applied.

The data in this chapter also suggest that the nature of stressors influences what families find helpful and how often the strategies are helpful. The families coping with bankruptcy, for instance, consistently found the various strategies less helpful than the families coping with the other stressors. This implies that this stressor is qualitatively different than the others included in our research, and it tends to require different types of stress-management strategies. In some instances, the infertility group also revealed unique findings, suggesting that this is also a relatively unique stressor.

Most of the strategies in our project were found to be generally helpful by the majority of respondents. However, even the most useful strategies are not universally helpful. All were harmful in some situations. The best conclusion is that several constructive strategies tend to be helpful to the majority of families a majority of the time and in a wide range of stressful situations. Also, some stress-management strategies are helpful more frequently than others. And some tend to be harmful most of the time.

NINE

Developmental Patterns in Family Coping

The purpose of this chapter is to test part of the systemic theory developed in Chapter 3. The theory was explained in detail in that chapter, but it seems useful to briefly summarize here the part of the theory that is being tested.

LEVELS I, II, AND III COPING STRATEGIES

The theory proposed that when families are experiencing stress they tend to go through a sequential process of trying Level I coping strategies first. If the Level I strategies successfully manage the stress, then a family does not tend to use the more abstract coping strategies. The criterion that determines whether the strategies are successful is whether the family believes that its new rules of transformation adequately deal with the previously threatening inputs well enough that the system outputs meet the family's standards.

Level I strategies are attempts to change specific and observable behaviors and rules in the family system. For example, families may try to change rules about when members of the family must be home and what the responsibilities of family members are. They may try to rearrange their roles. They may seek help from relatives and friends to find out what they have done in similar situations, or they may seek new information from professional sources to try to determine what kinds of relatively minor changes they can make to deal with the threatening inputs (stressor events).

In situations where the Level I coping strategies are not able to cope adequately with the threatening inputs, several predictable processes tend to occur. Families find themselves still in a stressful situation, and it usually is a deeper and more serious form of stress than when the family was trying Level I strategies. Families then turn to more abstract coping strategies. Level II strategies are more complex and abstract than Level I because they deal with such things as the family regime (Constantine, 1986), the metarules (rules about the family's rules of transformation), and other fundamental aspects of the system's basic organization.

These strategies can include such things as reviewing decision-making methods, changing the method of family governance, and changing the way it makes and changes rules. The strategies also may involve the structure of core systemic processes such as trying to communicate in different ways, being more or less loving, being more or less supportive, and changing the amount of cooperation versus competition.

The theory suggests that when these Level II strategies are successful in coping with the threatening inputs, the family tends to not resort to Level III strategies. However, when the Level II strategies do not adequately cope with the stress, there are attempts to change the fundamental assumptions, values, or philosophy of life that guide the family. Reiss (1981) coined the term *family paradigms* to describe these framing beliefs.

The purpose of the research discussed in this chapter is to test the idea that this developmental sequence occurs in the way families cope with stress. The specific research objectives are to determine if the families in our sample passed through a sequential process from Level I to Level II to Level III strategies. We also were interested in seeing if the developmental pattern existed with certain types of stressors and not with others, as well as whether families experiencing some types of stressors tend to go straight to Level II or III strategies.

METHODOLOGY

A modified Q-sort was used to gather data that would help us test these questions about developmental patterns of managing stress. Cards were created for each of the 80 coping strategies discussed in Chapter 7. Couples were asked to work together to decide which of the strategies were used at which times during the process of managing their stressful situation. Before the sorting process began with each couple, the cards were shuffled by the interviewer so that the sorting process would not be biased by the order of the cards.

Before the pilot interviews, the plan for the Q-sort was to have six categories into which the couple could sort the strategies:

1. Never used it,
2. immediately used it,
3. soon—but not immediately,
4. in the middle of the process,
5. very late in the process, and
6. all during the process.

However, during the training interviews, we found that nearly all of the cards were being placed in the "all during the process" category rather than the other categories. Because there would be little variability if most of the cards were in one category, we decided to eliminate the "all during" category. In subsequent interviews, the couples were asked to sort the 80 coping strategies in the remaining five categories based on when they first started using the strategies.

This part of the interview was seen as a couples activity, because they were asked to do the sorting together. In households with solo parents, the individual did the sorting activity alone.

Discrepancies occurred sometimes between husbands and wives; when they did, the couples were asked to come to an agreement as to whether the strategy was important and when they thought the person or family began to use it. In many situations a brief discussion led to what seemed to be a comfortable consensus. In other situations, only one individual had used the strategy, and the individual usually placed it where he or she thought it should go. In some situations, however, the couples did not resolve their disagreements, and we needed to recognize they had different opinions. Sometimes, if they decided that it really did not matter to the individual who used that strategy, they placed the card in the "never used it" pile.

The interviewers were involved with the couples as they completed their Q-sort. We tried to be helpful rather than intrusive or interfering. We found ourselves interpreting what we were after when the couples did not understand, and we tried to help clarify ambiguous situations. Our goal was to try to understand what had happened in their families, and generally they seemed appreciative of us participating with them in a collaborative way.

We used both qualitative and quantitative methods in analyzing the data. We evaluated the transcripts and our notes in the qualitative part of the analysis. In the quantitative part, the data were coded by using each of the 80 coping strategies as variables and assigning a value according to the categories under which the strategy was placed for each couple. Because of the similarity in time frame of the immediately and soon categories, they were combined into one category called "Early." This left us with three time periods during the coping: early, in the middle, and very late in the process of coping.

Before we analyzed the data, we classified the 80 strategies according to whether they were attempts to make Level I, II, or III changes. This process turned out to be more difficult than we expected because some of the strategies could be viewed as being in more than one category. The method we used was to have three members of the research team individually categorize the strategies. Most of the strategies were labeled as the same level of abstraction by all three researchers, but some discrepancies existed. We found that the differences between Levels I and III were easy to identify, but it was difficult to determine if some of the strategies should be viewed as Levels I or II. Several strategies seemed to be on the border between Levels I and II. We initially labeled the vague strategies as Level II-A and those that more clearly involved Level II change were labeled II-B.

Another refinement we made before analysis was eliminating so-called negative strategies such as denial and trying to forget the event. Combining frequencies for unhelpful strategies (which very few people used) with frequencies of helpful strategies did not seem to make sense. Our goal was to examine the developmental patterns of useful and helpful coping strategies in terms of the three levels of abstraction; including the negative strategies seemed to add a confusing extra dimension.

The sample also was slightly smaller for this part of the data analysis. Only 44 families completed all of the Q-sort because some did not get to it or we felt that our welcome ran out before this part of the interview.

RESULTS AND DISCUSSION

Sequences in Using the Levels of Analysis

The data were analyzed quantitatively by looking at how frequently the various strategies were used at the different stages of stress management. We initially made a very large table that showed the percentage of families using each strategy in the three process stages—early, middle, and late. Table 9.1 summarizes this information by showing the average percentage of strategy use.

The descriptive information in this table provides new and interesting information. It shows that families tended to use approximately half of the strategies we studied early in their coping. Between 25% and 30% of the total strategies were tried for the first time in the middle stages of the coping, and 16% to 23% of the strategies were not tried until late in the coping.

Table 9.1 also has differences that are consistent with the theoretical predictions. The Level I strategies were used the most in the early stage (60%) and the least in the late stage (16%). Also, the Level III strategies were used the least in the early stage and the most in the late stage.

To determine whether these differences were statistically significant, we combined the Levels II-A and II-B categories and computed a Chi-square test. Table 9.2 shows the cross-tabulation of the

Table 9.1 Percentage Using Strategies From Levels I, II, and III

Levels	Early (%)	Middle (%)	Late (%)
Level I	60	24	16
Level II-A	53	30	17
Level II-B	49	31	20
Level II Total	52	30	18
Level III	48	29	23

Table 9.2 Cross-Tabulation of Abstraction Levels and Timing of Use and Chi-Square Statistic

Level of Abstraction	Early Observed (Expected)	Middle Observed (Expected)	Late Observed (Expected)	Total
Level I	1,001 (966.17)	397 (419.32)	266 (279.51)	1,664
Level II	166 (186.96)	98 (81.14)	58 (53.89)	322
Level III	68 (81.87)	41 (35.53)	32 (23.60)	141
Total	1,235	536	356	2,127

$\chi^2 = 15.35$, $df = 4$, $p < .01$.

total use of the three levels of coping strategies and the three categories of early, middle, and late. The Chi-square was statistically significant ($\chi^2 = 15.35$, $p < .01$). This provides some support for the theoretical idea of a developmental sequence in the way families use the three levels of coping strategies.

In addition to this quantitative analysis, we also looked at the data qualitatively to better determine developmental patterns and their characteristics. Our qualitative analysis revealed that many of the families moved through the developmental sequence as the theory predicted. For example, a comment made by a couple experiencing infertility shows how they used the strategy of gaining more knowledge (a Level I strategy) early on. "At first we tried to approach it from getting more knowledge on the situation. We took classes at the university and I bought books. . . . That helped to an extent. At least you felt like you knew what you were talking about. I think that helped us get a little more in control at first."

Another couple dealing with infertility is an example of the use of Level III strategies late in the process. They said they changed their basic values and reexamined their basic beliefs quite late in the process. When asked whether values had changed, the husband replied, "I think that our values have changed to a certain extent. In one sense, I think that we have even a higher value that we place upon life, so that we're willing to invest more of our resources just trying to be able to have a chance of having a family."

When we began the project, we wondered how much the families would use Level III strategies. Later, as we evaluated the transcripts, we observed that a substantial number of them changed some of their life philosophies and values while dealing with their particular stressful situation. One family with an institutionalized handicapped child said, "Material things don't mean as much. Family and religion have become more important. Puts things in perspective. We appreciate our life, health, happiness more."

Another couple dealing with muscular dystrophy said that they changed their values to become more sensitive, caring, and kind as a result of their stress. Another woman said that her faith in God became stronger because of her handicapped child.

Some families who experienced the other stressors of infertility, bankruptcy, displaced homemaker, or troubled teen also had substantial changes in their basic philosophies. Some said they turned more to religious beliefs, greater faith in God, or greater activity in their church. A couple experiencing infertility found that strengthening their faith in God was their most important and helpful strategy. Another common theme was that people said they valued both their families and their relationships with other people more. One partner in a couple dealing with bankruptcy said, "I think I learned to try and be satisfied with what I have. . . . It made me realize what really counts in life. When we die, what will we have? It's not our cars and our home. It's our family. That's all there is in life is our family. All we had was our kids and each other. That's pretty humbling. You start thinking, 'Wow! What's really important?' Actually, it's people and relationships, friends and family."

Other values or philosophies about life that changed had to do with how families related to other people. For example, one partner of a couple that experienced bankruptcy said, "I don't think any of our basic values have changed as far as religion or family relationships or stuff like that. The basic philosophy of life has changed somewhat, where before we were somewhat passive and timid actually, and we would probably let people intimidate us more, we don't put up with that anymore."

A displaced homemaker stated that she had felt unable to control her life, decisions, or her feelings and that going through this stressful situation helped her to "take control and decide to take responsibility . . . over [her] life."

Many of the families, regardless of the type of stressor, discussed how religious values were important to them, and how they found themselves relying on their beliefs more as they dealt with the stress. Many of the families who appeared to go through a paradigm shift—that is, a change in their basic philosophies and values—said that these changes were helpful in managing the stress. One woman with a handicapped child stated that because of her religious convictions, she only sees the good that came out of her situation, because "I believe this happened to me and my family to make us learn and grow and to make us love each other more. . . . We'll grow from it. I think it's to our advantage."

However, some families did not go through Level III changes while dealing with the stress. A couple with a child with muscular dystrophy stated that they never really changed their philosophy, beliefs, or values.

Generally, our qualitative analysis suggested that when families made Level III changes, they did not do it early in the process of coping. They found themselves struggling with complex situations for a period of time, and the changes were neither quick nor easy. Some Level III changes occurred relatively early in the process of coping, but most seemed to occur slowly and gradually and after a period of struggling with less abstract strategies. The patterns, however, were complex, and the changes did not fit the theory in a common and clear-cut pattern. There was great variation even in our small sample. The patterns that we did find show the value of approaching the issue from a different perspective. We believe that our findings provide a slim thread for learning more about the developmental nature of family stress and how families change what they do during the process of coping. Several families also showed how they used Level II strategies in the middle of the coping. A couple with a muscular dystrophic child said they tried to increase family togetherness by traveling together as a family in the middle of the process when their child was old enough and yet still mobile enough to enjoy the travels. An infertile couple said they changed the "way they made decisions" during the middle of dealing with their infertility.

To summarize, our qualitative and quantitative analysis both provide some evidence that the developmental sequence idea has merit. Our intuitive and qualitative analysis probably provided more evidence than the quantitative analysis. It is important, however, to realize that these tests of this theoretical idea are limited, and the discernible differences were not universal. Therefore, more research is needed before we can conclude that developmental patterns exist in the way families use coping strategies.

We also should realize that this theoretical idea only provides a little bit of understanding about when and why families use the strategies they do. There is considerable variation in the developmental pattern. The families in our sample began to use Level III strategies early in their coping 52% of the time, and they did not use some Level I strategies until late in their coping 16% of the time.

In addition, there is much more variability as to when strategies are used than Table 9.1 shows. There only the average percentage of time each level of strategies were used is shown. The table does not show the variation that occurred within each cell. Some strategies were used by almost all families at one particular time in the development of the stressful situation. For example, the Level I items "Tried to seek additional information" and "Tried to accept the situation" were used early 82% and 80% of the time, respectively.

Some other strategies were initially used by families about equally in the different stages. For example, the Level II item "Tried to develop more trusting relationships with others" and the Level III item "Changed basic 'philosophy of life' as a result of this situation" were used approximately 25% of the time in all three stages.

These exceptions to the predicted theoretical pattern led us to examine the data in another way to learn more about when the developmental pattern does and does not appear. This additional analysis is presented in the following section.

Using Levels of Abstraction According to Stressors

One way of learning more about the developmental pattern is to see if it was different according to the type of stressor the families were managing. It may be that the developmental pattern appears more clearly with certain stressful situations and less clearly with others. Also, it is possible that some stressful situations may necessitate the use of higher-level coping strategies more than do other stressors.

Table 9.3 shows the total frequencies and percentages of use for each of the six stressors that were studied in this research project. The percentages in the table are helpful in looking at the differences in the use of the coping strategies from the three levels of abstraction for each stressor because the numbers of families in each category are different.

A pattern can be seen in Table 9.3 that seems to provide new information about when the theorized developmental pattern does and does not occur. The developmental sequence seems to be stronger among displaced homemakers and families dealing with bankruptcy, infertility, and troubled teens. These four stressors also seem to be somewhat more acute. Even though they often occurred over several years, they do not seem likely to carry on through many years. For example, the sample of bankrupt families and the displaced homemakers appeared to have managed their situations during a 2- or 3-year period. Infertility may not seem like an acute stressor because it can last for many years. However, in this sample, most of the infertile couples had been dealing with it for 5 or fewer years.

The other two stressors, families with handicapped institutionalized children and children with muscular dystrophy, are more chronic. Having children with such disabilities as multiple handicaps or muscular dystrophy are stressors that last for many years.

Table 9.3 Use of Levels of Abstraction by Stressor

Institutionalized Handicapped Child								
Levels of	*Never*		*Early*		*Middle*		*Late*	
Abstraction	%	N	%	N	%	N	%	N
Level I	26	137	47	251	18	95	9	48
Level II	31	29	45	43	20	21	3	3
Level III	56	18	22	7	19	6	3	1
Muscular Dystrophy								
Levels of	*Never*		*Early*		*Middle*		*Late*	
Abstraction	%	N	%	N	%	N	%	N
Level I	39	226	41	234	13	75	7	42
Level II	40	43	30	32	22	24	8	9
Level III	44	16	36	13	17	6	3	1
Bankruptcy								
Levels of	*Never*		*Early*		*Middle*		*Late*	
Abstraction	%	N	%	N	%	N	%	N
Level I	45	207	32	148	14	64	9	39
Level II	29	24	35	29	14	12	22	19
Level III	39	11	11	3	29	8	21	6
Infertility								
Levels of	*Never*		*Early*		*Middle*		*Late*	
Abstraction	%	N	%	N	%	N	%	N
Level I	25	145	47	273	16	94	12	68
Level II	27	29	33	36	27	29	14	13
Level III	39	14	19	7	17	6	25	9

Many of the families interviewed had children with disabilities that were at least 10 years old and often much older. The developmental sequence in the use of strategies from the three levels of abstraction is not seen as clearly in these two stressors. Using particular coping strategies from the three levels of abstraction does not seem to be related to the development of the process over the years. In fact, the pattern almost looks like most of the strategies were used early on in the process, regardless of the level of abstraction.

Thus we believe that a new generalization is justified by these data: The developmental pattern suggested by Burr (1989) tends to occur more clearly when stressful situations in family systems are of a relatively acute nature. The developmental pattern does not seem to appear when family systems are coping with long-term, chronic stressors.

One reason that the pattern of the developmental sequence of coping strategies is not found with more chronic stressors could be that for these families who have dealt with a problem for so long, their perception of the category of "early" is much longer than for families dealing with acute stressors. For someone with an 18-year-old child with muscular dystrophy, anything before the child was 12 may be considered early in the process.

Families dealing with stressors that last only a couple of years probably define *early, middle,* and *late* much more easily. Families dealing with handicapped children may actually go through developmental processes of using strategies from the three levels of abstraction, but the crude measurement we used was not able to identify the patterns. When couples were asked simply to say when they first started using a strategy, the pattern of development may have all occurred within the first few months or years of dealing with their problem. Information would have been lost because they would have sorted the cards into the early category.

Another possible reason why the developmental pattern is not as strong for the chronic situations may be because of the nature of the children's illness. Maybe these families go through the pattern of levels every time something new occurs to their children that creates new stress. For example, one couple with a muscular dystrophic child said that for some seven years they went through a pattern of living normally and then having to deal with the developments of the disease, which caused familial and emotional disruption for a while. After they were used to each new development, they could live somewhat normally again until another major development occurred. "Each time there was this new step, we had to go through the emotions again and readjust—'How are we going to keep him going this time?'—and work with it. So it was a periodic thing where every 6 months or 9 months this deterioration occurred until the last 2 years of his life."

Another family with a child with muscular dystrophy had similar experiences. They could function quite normally for a time, and then they would have to pass again through the stages of acceptance. "Each stage that you go through—if you put them in braces or put them in a wheelchair—your emotions and your family's functioning and everything that you consider a family unit does not operate as well."

Therefore, as these families stated, they go through the stages of managing the stress of a handicapped child several times over the years of dealing with the illness. In between these stages, their life becomes somewhat normal or at least they learn to view it as normal. The pattern of going through the different levels of abstraction in the use of their strategies may be still be present in families dealing with chronic situations, but the pattern may occur every time the families need to deal with a new aspect of the problem. Thus the nature of the children's illness—continuous deterioration—may lead to repeated use of different levels of coping.

Another possible reason why the developmental pattern does not appear to exist is that having a chronically disabled child may be a stressor that actually hits the core of the family system very early in the stressful situation process. Many of these families may go through changes to their family system and family paradigms because of the stress's severity. The chronic and severe nature of the stressors that we studied may necessitate the use of Level III strategies because families are dealing with core beliefs about life and death. Possibly, some families have to deal with Level III issues almost immediately when they have such a severe problem as a handicapped child, leading to the difficulty we had of seeing a developmental pattern with these two stressors.

To summarize, the developmental pattern postulated by our theory is found among families dealing with relatively acute stressful situations. The developmental pattern does not occur in quite the same way when families are dealing with more chronic problems. We suspect that some of the reasons for this difference are:

- the length of time dealing with the problem may change the families' perceptions of early, middle, and late so that they are different from those of families with acute stressors;
- the degenerative nature of the illness may have led to the pattern repeating itself over the years; and
- the severity of the problem may necessitate Level III coping early in the process.

LIMITATIONS OF THIS RESEARCH

One limitation to the study of the developmental pattern of the use of strategies from three levels of abstraction is the crudeness of the measurement. The Q-sort did show some differences between the use of strategies from the three levels, as seen in the chi-square and other analyses above. However, simply sorting strategies into categories according to when they were used does not seem to show the possible developmental patterns that might occur several times over a long period of chronic situations. A more accurate measurement is needed for a better understanding of how people deal with their new problems, disappointments, or deteriorations. If people were asked to think about what they did within each stage of the stressful process, they would show that they actually do follow developmental patterns in using (a) Level I strategies, (b) Level II strategies, and (c) Level III strategies if they are needed.

Another limitation of our measurement and analysis is that we did not ask families if they decided to try more abstract strategies when they found that using strategies from a lower level of abstraction did not help. There may be a way to tell the couples which strategies belonged to each level and then have them first sort Level I strategies according to time of use and whether they found those strategies helpful or not; they then could be asked whether they continued on to the strategies from other levels.

A final limitation in this chapter is that we included an overabundance of Level I strategies and few Level II and III strategies. Part of the reason for this was that most of the strategies listed in the previous research were Level I. We could find few Level II and III strategies in the literature. It may have been better to limit the Level I strategies somewhat to avoid such an imbalance in the assessment of the three levels. We hope that these limitations will be dealt with more adequately in future research.

CONCLUSION

This study is the first of its kind and sought to establish whether a developmental pattern exists in the use of coping strategies from the three levels of abstraction. Because it is such a new area, the study has barely scratched the surface of research possibilities. The study has several limitations, some noted and others perhaps yet to be identified. Despite the limitations, evidence does exist that developmental patterns are present in the use of Level I, II, and III strategies, as our theory proposed. Clearly, these findings warrant further study and replication.

T E N

General Principles, Implications, and Future Directions

Our goals in this chapter are to generalize, integrate, and evaluate. We will summarize the way the data support principles that have been suggested in earlier literature, propose new principles, describe the implications these ideas have for practitioners, and make recommendations for future research.

THE SEARCH FOR PRINCIPLES

This research was guided by a paradigmatic orientation that seeks general principles. However, before we can identify useful principles, we need a foundation of conceptual ideas and descriptive research. This project is mostly a contribution to these underpinnings: Our main goals have been conceptual improvement and description of processes. The conceptual improvements included a systemic approach that is more internally consistent and fruitful than previous models. We also proposed a conceptual framework of coping strategies, as well as proposed a developmental sequence in the process of coping.

We used these conceptual tools to gather descriptive data about family processes. We described several new patterns in the way family systems respond to stressful times. We also described how multiple aspects of the family system respond to stress and looked at how families, and the men and women in those families, use coping strategies to deal with stress. We also discovered new information about the proportion of families who found various coping strategies helpful and harmful, and we found evidence of a developmental pattern in the way families use coping strategies.

We initially assumed these conceptual improvements and new descriptive data would allow us to generate general principles. As we conclude this project, we are impressed with how much additional conceptual and descriptive work there is yet to do and how difficult it is to develop such principles.

We still believe the construction of general principles is an important agenda for family researchers. The family stress literature is a large body of literature that has been accumulating since the 1930s, and yet this area has not yielded very many such general principles that are helpful to families or to those who help families.

This is quite different from some of the other content areas in family science where we have a larger number of helpful generalizations. For example, we have developed a large number of helpful principles about correlates of marital satisfaction and acquired a large number of helpful generalizations about parent-child relationships and the family emotional system (Kerr & Bowen, 1988). With family stress, however, we have a different situation. We have hundreds of studies and study reviews, yet we have relatively few general principles. Most of the research has led to typologies, descriptive information, and correlation studies that deal with how fairly static variables are associated with the amount of crisis. The research has not led to the accumulation of a comparable set of principles that are helpful to families and those who try to help families.

Complexity of Family Responses

Even though the present study was primarily conceptual and descriptive, several aspects of the data move us closer to general principles. One of these generalizations is that the process of coping with stress in family systems is more complex and variable than most of the previous literature in the field has suggested. Walker's (1985) paper argued on conceptual grounds that these processes are more complex than our theories were appreciating. Also, Boss's (1987) volume moved us in the direction of appreciating greater complexity. Our data provide evidence that these processes are even more complex and variable.

Some of our data that argue for this generalization are that there are many more response patterns than we previously realized, different parts of family systems respond differently during the process of stress, and the strategies for coping have variable effects in families. Even the strategies that seem intuitively useful and have been empirically tested are harmful in some circumstances. Further, strategies that are generally thought to be harmful are helpful 25% of the time. In addition, the events that input stress into family systems have many differences. Various stressors lead to different changes in families and demand different management strategies.

This generalization about the complexity and variability in the way families respond to stress leads to the following principle.

PRINCIPLE: When family systems experience stress, the changes that result are extremely complex and varied.

In our project, we were not able to pay attention systematically to many of the factors that add additional layers of complexity and variability to what happens during family stress. In our project, we ignored racial and ethnic differences. We also ignored differences in such basic demographic conditions as education, social status, age, family composition, and life-style. These factors undoubtedly contribute to additional complexity and variability, and other less homogeneous samples may be even more complex and varied.

Thus this study argues that if we are to gain a more comprehensive, accurate, and useful understanding of family stress, then it will help if we move to models that will be more sensitive to the diversity and variability of the phenomena being studied. We hope the conceptual and theoretical improvements we have suggested will facilitate this. The ABC-X models were useful in earlier decades, and they may continue to be useful in some ways in the future, but they are restrictive models in the sense that they try to minimize uniqueness and simplify very complex phenomena. The systems model is more open-ended and sensitive to the variability in families. In fact, we suspect that the change in the theoretical lenses we used was one reason this study was able to detect the variability we found.

This principle has several implications for family practitioners. It suggests that family functioning can remain constant or even improve in the midst of severely stressful experiences. The previous literature has recognized that families may be better off after they recover from a stressful situation, but we have underappreciated the variation in how families respond. Family scientists have thought of a decline in family functioning as inevitably linked with stress. Efforts have been directed at determining how deep and how long the decline might be and what is involved in recovery. These efforts are important, but we are now aware that this is only one of several response patterns.

Models such as the roller-coaster pattern are useful because they tell families what they can expect and what is normal. Our study adds evidence to the proposition that Koos's roller-coaster model of family stress is frequently valid but that it describes what families go through only half the time when they deal with severe stressors. Our research broadens our insights into what is normal, and it offers different expectations to those who suffer. We also observed four other models operating in the families we studied: the increased, no change, decreased, and mixed models. These findings can help families and those who work with families be aware that there are several normal ways to respond to stress.

Early Response to Stress

A second tentative principle also stems from the generalization about complexity and variability in family response patterns to stress. Our data tentatively suggest that family systems have the same five ways of responding to stress even though the stressors change. Our data also suggest only minor gender differences in responses to stress. However, the more serious the situation, the more likely the family will experience a decline in quality of functioning.

Also, several patterns of resource allocation were evident: Slightly less than half the families reported an increase in energy expenditure as family functioning declined. Other families had different responses, again reminding us of the complexity and variability of family responses to stress. In general, timing tended to lag, but families who recognized the stress quickly and took steps to alleviate it early in the process of responding reported more positive patterns of family functioning. Thus our data suggest the following principle.

PRINCIPLE: Families that allocate resources to a stressful situation relatively quickly rather than wait tend to cope more effectively.

Apparently, families who have an early and considerable allocation of resources such as their time, effort, and energy to the stressful situation tend to have more positive response patterns. This is a finding that should be viewed as tentative until it is replicated in additional research, but it suggests that families who dally in dealing with their difficult situations tend to pay a greater price. Folklore versions of this principle—"A stitch in time saves nine" and "An ounce of prevention is worth a pound of cure"—have long suggested this idea. Moving the idea toward a principle is action long past due.

Coping With Emotions

Previous research has found that it is helpful if families focus on the management of emotions during stressful periods (Boss, 1987; McCubbin & Figley, 1983; McCubbin & Dahl, 1985). The data in this study add evidence to this generalization, and it may be that we ought to elevate this idea to the status of a principle.

PRINCIPLE: If families focus on the unusual changes in their emotional systems during periods of family stress, then they tend to cope more effectively.

Several aspects of this study argue for the validity of this principle. Our data showed that the emotional climate in family systems
was disrupted more frequently—85% of the time—than any other
aspect of family systems. Also, the emotionally focused coping
strategies were among the most helpful strategies, and some of the
most harmful strategies were the inappropriate emotional strategies.

This principle has several important implications for practitioners. It identifies an area in which families can expect to be usually
disrupted, and it can be helpful if families are aware of the likelihood that the emotional part of their family system usually is disrupted. It also could be helpful to many families to learn that it is
not usually irreparably damaging to have emotional disruption.
Rather, the disruption in this part of family systems is a fairly predictable and normal part of the stress processes and tends to pass.

Another implication of this principle is that it suggests a place
where families apparently will benefit from focusing their efforts.
Apparently, if families try to manage their negative emotions so
they do not aggravate the stressful situation, it helps. Also, if they
try to create feelings of optimism, closeness, a spirit of oneness,
these positive feelings also usually help families cope with stressful situations.

Family Stress Often Has a Silver Lining

The data in this study also document another generalization that
is based on the fact that different family subsystems respond differently during family stress. The emotional subsystem almost always responds in a roller-coaster fashion when significant stress
makes its appearance, but other aspects of family systems tend to
not be impaired by stress. Also, some aspects of family systems
frequently improve during family stress.

The data suggest that the parts of family systems that are the
most likely to improve are family communication, cohesion, bond-
ing, and togetherness. Thus family stress should not be viewed as
a doom-and-gloom occurrence to be avoided at all costs. It apparently also tends to improve some things as families are constrained
to unite in their efforts to overcome the potential negative effects
of the stressor.

If families were more aware of this silver lining aspect of family stress, then it might improve the morale and coping effectiveness of many families. It may alleviate some of the emotions that disrupt, and it may help create feelings that a family can do what is needed, including prioritizing goals and values and communicating and listening more intently.

Consistent Coping Strategies

Another principle that can be drawn from our data has to do with differences in the types of stressors and the way families respond in different ways. The patterns revealed by our data suggest there tend to be some differences in stressors that families ought to consider as they try to cope with their situations.

The families coping with bankruptcy found some strategies less helpful than the families coping with the other stressors. This implies that this type of stressor is qualitatively different from the others included in our research, and it tends to require different types of stress-management strategies. This finding reinforces Foa's (1971) idea that different strategies are helpful in economic situations and in interpersonal situations. In some instances the infertility group also revealed unique findings, suggesting that this is also a relatively unique stressor. These data suggest the following principle.

PRINCIPLE: If families that are experiencing stress recognize that appropriate coping strategies are available, then they may be able to cope more effectively.

This principle also has several implications for practitioners. For example, we can identify a large number of strategies that are widely used and generally helpful. The strategies that were included in this research were used some 75% of the time and were helpful 80% of the time. Including this information in family life education material may help families broaden their repertoires of strategies.

Our data also suggest that different stressful situations need somewhat different coping strategies. Families who are coping

with financial problems such as bankruptcy do not find the interpersonal and emotional strategies as helpful as families who are
coping with more interpersonal and intangible stressors.

Variation in the Helpfulness of Coping Strategies

Figley and McCubbin (1983) identified a list of coping strategies
that they believed were "universal characteristics which differentiate functional and dysfunctional coping" (p. 18). McCubbin and
Dahl (1985) also identified several coping strategies that tend to be
harmful to families.

Our data provide several refinements to the idea that these strategies are universally helpful or harmful. Again, the first principle
about diversity and variability is relevant. The family realm exhib-
its wide variation, and families differ considerably in how they use
coping strategies. This idea is, of course, not new with this research. It is a theme that has been emphasized in many different
places in the family literature (Constantine, 1986; Reiss, 1981;
Walker, 1985).

Two principles seem to be defensible about this part of our data
with regard to coping strategies.

PRINCIPLE: If families use coping strategies that are generally thought
             to be harmful, then the strategies are harmful most of the
             time but helpful some of the time.

PRINCIPLE: If families use coping strategies that are generally thought
             to be helpful (such as focusing on spiritual, communication,
             emotional, and cohesion aspects of family life), then they
             are helpful most of the time but harmful some of the time.

Most of the helpful coping strategies were found to be helpful
most of the time by the majority of respondents. However, our
findings suggest that these strategies are not universal in a literal
sense. Even the most helpful strategies are harmful in some situations. We should probably be more cautious and tentative than
McCubbin and Figley's claim that these strategies are "universal
and transcend all . . . stressors." Hopefully, future research will

help us better understand the conditions under which the various coping strategies are helpful and harmful.

Many aspects of our data argue for these two principles. For example, in our data all of the coping strategies were useful in some way or another. This suggests that not one set of universally good coping strategies or a small set of coping strategies are the main or key strategies.

Also, our subjects found that the most frequently used strategies focused on spiritual parts of life, communication processes, the emotional subsystem, and family cohesion. Less frequently used strategies focused on cognitive processes and seeking resources in the community. This suggests that even though a wide range of strategies is useful in coping with family stress, some strategies are more useful.

One interesting aspect of our data is that the spiritual strategies tend to be helpful more than most other kinds of strategies. This finding is quite different from the impression that is created by the scholarly literature on family stress. The scholarly literature has emphasized the rational components of cognitive strategies such as defining and redefining and the processes of seeking help from the community. Ironically, our data suggest that these two kinds of coping strategies are the least useful of all. And, at the other extreme, spiritual strategies that have been deemphasized and even neglected in the literature are among the most useful strategies.

It is possible that our finding about the high helpfulness of the spiritual strategies is somewhat unique to our sample. Our sample mostly included members of the Church of Jesus Christ Latter-day Saints (LDS) or Mormons. On the other hand, it may not be a sampling characteristic because the same pattern occurred with the non-LDS families in our sample, and we doubt that merely living in the Rocky Mountains makes the spiritual part of life more important.

As part of our interviews we asked each family what it did that helped the most in coping with its situation. A large proportion of these families' comments dealt with the spiritual part of their lives—and it was the spiritual comments that were the most animated and emphatic. This finding is consistent with other recent research about family stress. Ladewig, Jessee, and Strickland (1992, p. 65) also found that spiritual support was "particularly helpful" in coping with the stress created when a child was held hostage.

These two principles have several practical implications. They suggest that practitioners ought to be sensitive to the diversity of families, the uniqueness of various family situations, and the contexts that are so different. Thus far we know little about the circumstances under which the various harmful strategies are helpful, but knowing they are helpful in a sizable minority of situations ought to help us be more tentative, cautious, and appreciative of the diversity in the family realm.

It is important to help families understand that not all coping strategies are helpful for everyone in every situation. There are many strategies that tend to be generally helpful, but there are also some strategies that could actually be harmful for them in their attempt to resolve their concerns. Professionals and others need to be sensitive to each family's specific concerns and needs and then provide the help that might be useful for their family situation.

A final point is that these ideas could be included in educational materials and classrooms, the development of mass media materials, and therapeutic settings. Fortunately, the communication, emotional, and cohesion aspects of families are included often in educational materials, enrichment programs (Dinkmeyer & Carlson, 1984; Gordon, 1970), and therapeutic approaches. With regard to the ideas about spiritual strategies, many believe our society is becoming more secular, which it undoubtedly is in many ways. If we were to rely on what is included in the mass media and the academic community generally, we could reasonably conclude that the spiritual part of life is generally quite irrelevant, indefensible, and only relevant for those who have not learned how to rely on the more defensible rational processes. Our data suggest that many families find the spiritual part of their life meaningful and helpful as they try to manage stressful situations.

Gender Differences

One final idea about coping strategies is that our data suggest that men and women use coping strategies a little differently. The data suggest that many women tend to reach out a little more and that many men tend to withdraw and go it alone. This pattern also has been found in other literature. Levenson and Gottman (1983, 1985) and Carstensen, Morrow, and Roberts (1991) found distinct patterns of emotional expressiveness between husbands and wives. Women tended to be more emotionally expressive and used strategies that helped them focus their emotions, while men tended to dampen their emotions and use more distracting, avoidance-type strategies to cope with their emotions. These findings offer a slim thread on which to suggest the following principle.

PRINCIPLE: If families and practitioners are sensitive to gender differences during family stress, they will tend to be more effective.

Developmental Patterns

This research also provides a little information about the type of stressors that tend to involve first-, second-, or third-order change in families. The theory and data suggest that families tend to use Level I strategies more extensively early in the stress process and Level II or III strategies later. Apparently, this pattern is more clear when families have more acute stressors than chronic stressors. The developmental pattern is obscured when families are coping with chronic stressors, such as having a handicapped or chronically ill child, because the coping goes on for a longer period of time.

It may be that if families or practitioners are aware of this developmental pattern, then they can be more helpful to families. However, our knowledge of these processes is so preliminary that it would be premature to try identifying any principles or more useful generalizations.

RECOMMENDATIONS FOR FUTURE RESEARCH

As we end our study, we realize more acutely how much we still do not know about families in stress. We still must learn more about how systemic processes change and remain the same in different ethnic, racial, religious, and cultural settings. And before we will have very many useful principles, we need to learn more about how different types of stressful inputs have differing impacts on family systems and demand different types of responses.

We also have formed an opinion about one type of research that we think will move us toward acquiring general principles. Such research would have several characteristics. First, it would differentiate between families who are and are not managing stress effectively and identify differences in the strategies they use. Second, it would not just identify the specific aspects of these differences, it would abstract and generalize to find a few general phenomena that differentiate them and that could be used as the basis for constructing principles. Third, it would identify the contextual factors that are related to when and how the various general strategies are and are not helpful. For example, as Foa (1971) suggested, different strategies may be helpful in economic and noneconomic situations. Also, as suggested in Chapter 8 of this volume, it may be that different strategies are helpful in chronic and acute situations, and there may be racial, ethnic, developmental, gender, religious, and cultural factors that may be contingencies. In retrospect, we wish we had the time and resources to pay attention to which families did well and poorly not only to identify what seems to help, but also to determine what went beyond the scope and resources of this project. That type of research is clearly what is now needed.

IN CONCLUSION

The resilience we found in the families we studied was impressive. The respondents were families who experienced extreme types of stress, and yet we found remarkable evidence of the growth and gains they made as both individuals and families as they weathered the storms of stress. We are almost willing to say that families who experience stress successfully find new levels of satisfaction and fulfillment in their family lives. It is as if the storm strengths family members and leads them to appreciate more deeply the periods of calm. We were heartened to find such evidence.

References

Angell, R. C. (1936). *The family encounters the Depression* (pp. 14-16). Gloucester, MA: Peter Smith.

Auerswald, E. H. (1985). Thinking about thinking in family therapy. *Family Process, 24*, 1-12.

Auerswald, E. H. (1987). Epistemological confusion in family therapy and research. *Family Process, 26*, 317-330.

Bateson, G. (1972). *Steps to an ecology of mind.* New York: Ballantine.

Bateson, G. (1979). *Mind and nature: A necessary unity.* New York: Dutton.

Becvar, D. S., & Becvar, R. J. (1988). *Family therapy: A systemic integration.* Boston: Allyn & Bacon.

Beutler, I. F., Burr, W. R., Bahr, K. S., & Herrin, D. A. (1989). Theoretical implications of the uniqueness of the family realm. *Journal of Marriage and the Family, 51*, 805-829.

Blumer, H. (1962). Society as symbolic interaction. In A. Rose (Ed.), *Human behavior and social processes.* Boston: Houghton Mifflin.

Boss, P. G. (1975). *Psychological father absence and presence: A theoretical formulation for an investigation into family systems interaction.* Unpublished Ph.D. dissertation, University of Wisconsin, Madison, WI.

Boss, P. G. (1977). A clarification of the concept of psychological father presence in families experiencing ambiguity of boundary. *Journal of Marriage and the Family, 39*, 141-151.

Boss, P. (1987). Family stress. In M. B. Sussman & S. K. Steinmetz (Eds.), *Handbook of marriage and the family* (pp. 625-723). New York: Plenum.

Boss, P. (1988). *Family stress management.* Newbury Park, CA: Sage.

Boss, P., Doherty, W., LaRossa, R., & Schumm, W. (1992). *Sourcebook on marriage and the family.* New York: Plenum.

Boss, P. G., McCubbin, H. I., & Lester, G. (1979). The corporate executive wife's coping patterns in response to routine husband-father absence. *Family Process, 18*, 79-85.

Broderick, C. B. (1971). Beyond the five conceptual frameworks: A decade of development in family theory. *Journal of Marriage and the Family, 33*, 139-159.

Broderick, C., & Smith, J. (1979). The general systems approach to the family. In W. R. Burr, R. Hill, F. I. Nye, & I. L. Reiss (Eds.), *Contemporary theories about the family* (Vol. 2, pp. 112-129). New York: Free Press.

Bronfenbrenner, U. (1979). *The ecology of human development*. Cambridge, MA: Harvard University Press.

Brown, M., & Paolucci, B. (1979). *Home economics: A definition*. Washington DC: AHEA.

Buckley, W. (Ed.). (1968). *Modern systems research for the behavioral scientist*. Chicago: Aldine.

Burns, L. H. (1985). Infertility as boundary ambiguity: One theoretical perspective. *Family Process, 26*, 359-372.

Burr, R. G. (1983). *Reframing family stress theory: From the ABC-X model to a family ecosystemic model*. Unpublished master's thesis, Brigham Young University, Provo, UT.

Burr, W. R. (1973). *Theory construction and the sociology of the family*. New York: John Wiley.

Burr, W. R. (1976). *Successful marriage*. Homewood, IL: Dorsey.

Burr, W. R. (1991). Rethinking levels of abstraction in family systems theories. *Family Process, 30*, 435-453.

Burr, W. R., Day, R. D., & Bahr, K. S. (1993). *Family Science*. Belmont, CA: Brooks/Cole.

Burr, W. R., Hill, R., Nye, F. I., & Reiss, I. (Eds.). (1979). *Contemporary theories about the family* (Vol. 1). New York: Free Press.

Burr, W. R., Jensen, M., & Brady, L. (1977). A principles approach in family life education. *Family Coordinator, 26*, 225-233.

Caplan, G. (1964). *Principles of preventive psychiatry*. New York: Basic Books.

Capra, F. (1982). *The turning point*. New York: Simon & Schuster.

Carstensen, L. L., Morrow, J., & Roberts, T. (1991). *The experience of extreme emotion in romantic relationships*. Unpublished manuscript.

Cavan, R. S., & Ranck, K. H. (1938). *The family and the Depression*. Chicago: University of Chicago Press.

Christensen, H. T. (1964). *Handbook on marriage and the family*. Chicago: Rand McNally.

Constantine, L. L. (1986). *Family paradigms*. New York: Guilford.

Coomer, D. L., & Hultgren, F. H. (1989). Considering alternatives: An invitation to dialogue and question. In F. H. Hultgren (Ed.), *Alternative modes of inquiry*. Washington, DC: AHEA.

Davis, E. L., & Boss, P. G. (1980). *Rural divorce: How rural wives cope with separation*. Technical report. Madison, WI: Department of Child and Family Studies.

Deacon, R., & Firebaugh, F. M. (1986). *Home management: Context and concepts*. Boston: Houghton Mifflin.

Dinkmeyer, D., & Carlson, J. (1984). *Training in marriage enrichment*. Circle Pines, MN: American Guidance Service.

Doherty, W. (1986). Quanta, quarks, and families: Implications of quantum physics for family research. *Family Process, 25*, 249-263.

Duvall, E. R. (1955). *Family development*. Philadelphia: J. B. Lippincott.

Falicov, C. J. (1988). *Family transitions*. New York: Guilford.

Faulconer, J. E., & Williams, R. W. (1985). Temporality in human action: An alternative to positivism and historicism. *American Psychologist, 40*, 1119-1188.

Figley, C., & McCubbin, H. (Eds.). (1983). *Stress and the family: Coping with catastrophe* (Vol. 2). New York: Brunner/Mazel.

Foa, U. G. (1971). Interpersonal and economic resources. *Science, 171,* 345-351.

Fromm, E. (1941). *Escape from freedom.* New York: Rinehart.

Garbarino, J. (1982). *The individual and the family in a social context.* Hawthorne, NY: Aldine.

Gilbert, K. (1989). Interactive grief and coping in the marital dyad. *Death Studies, 13,* 605-626.

Gilligan, C. (1982). *In a different voice: Psychological theory and women's development.* Cambridge, MA: Harvard University Press.

Gordon, T. (1970). *Parent effectiveness training.* New York: Wyden.

Gouldner, V. (1988). Generation and gender: Normative and covert hierarchies. *Family Process, 27,* 17-31.

Gross, I. H., Crandall, E. W., & Knoll, M. M. (1980). *Management for modern families* (4th ed.). Englewood Cliffs, NJ: Prentice-Hall.

Habermas, J. (1972). *Knowledge and human interests.* Boston: Beacon.

Habermas, J. (1981). *The theory of communicative action* (Trans. by T. McCarthy). Boston: Beacon.

Hansen, D. A., & Hill, R. (1964). Families under stress. In H. T. Christensen (Ed.), *Handbook of marriage and the family.* Chicago: Rand McNally.

Hansen, D. A., & Johnson, V. A. (1979). Rethinking family stress theory: Definitional aspects. In W. R. Burr, R. Hill, F. I. Nye, & I. Reiss (Eds.), *Contemporary theories about the family* (Vol. 1, pp. 582-603). New York: Free Press.

Heidegger, M. (1962). *Being and time* (Trans. by J. Macquarrie & E. Robinson). New York: Harper & Row.

Hill, R. (1949). *Families under stress.* New York: Harper.

Hill, R. (1958). Generic features of families under stress. *Social Casework, 49,* 139-150.

Hill, R. (1971). Modern systems theory and the family: A confrontation. *Social Science Information, 10*(5), 7-26.

Hill, R., & Hansen, D. A. (1960). The identification of conceptual frameworks utilized in family study. *Marriage and Family Living, 22,* 199-311.

Hoffman, L. (1981). *Foundations of family therapy.* New York: Basic Books.

Holman, T. B., & Burr, W. R. (1980). Beyond the beyond: The growth of family theory in the 1970s. *Journal of Marriage and the Family, 41,* 729-735.

Holmes, T. H., & Rahe, R. H. (1967). The social readjustment rating scale. *Journal of Psychosomatic Research, 11,* 213-218.

Hultgren, F. H. (Ed.). (1989). *Alternative modes of inquiry,* Washington, DC: AHEA.

Jurich, J., & Burr, W. (1989). Valuing change. Paper presented at annual meeting of National Council on Family Relations, New Orleans, LA.

Kantor, D., & Lehr, W. (1975). *Inside the family.* San Francisco: Jossey-Bass.

Kaplan, D. M., Smith, A., Grobstein, R., & Fischman, S. E. (1973). Family mediation of stress. *Social Work, 18,* 60-69.

Keeney, B. P., & Sprenkle, D. H. (1982). Ecosystemic epistemology: Critical implications for the aesthetics and pragmatics of family therapy. *Family Process, 21,* 1-20.

Kerr, M. E., & Bowen, M. (1988). *Family evaluation: An approach based on Bowen theory.* New York: Norton.

Komorovsky, M. (1940). *The unemployed man and his family.* New York: Dryden.

Koos, E. L. (1946). *Families in trouble.* Morningside Heights, NY: King's Crown.

Kuhn, T. S. (1970). *The structure of scientific revolutions* (2nd ed.). Chicago: University of Chicago Press.

Ladewig, B. H., Jessee, P. O., & Strickland, M. P. (1992). Children held hostage: Mothers' depressive affect and perceptions of family psychosocial functioning. *Journal of Family Issues, 13*, 65-80.

Levenson, R. W., & Gottman, J. M. (1983). Marital interaction: Physiological linkage and affective exchange. *Journal of Personality and Social Psychology, 45*, 587-597.

Levenson, R. W., & Gottman, J. M. (1985). Physiological and affective predictors of change in relationship satisfaction. *Journal of Personality and Social Psychology, 49*, 85-94.

McCubbin, H. (1979). Integrating coping behavior in family stress theory. *Journal of Marriage and the Family, 41*, 237-244.

McCubbin, H., & Dahl, B. (1985). *Marriage and family: Individuals and life cycles.* New York: John Wiley.

McCubbin, H., Dahl, B., Lester, G., Benson, D., & Robertson, M. (1976). Coping repertoires of family adapting to prolonged war-induced separations. *Journal of Marriage and the Family, 38*, 471-478.

McCubbin, H., & Figley, C. (Eds.). (1983). *Stress and the family: Coping with normative transitions.* (Vol. 1). New York: Brunner/Mazel.

McCubbin, H., Joy, C., Cauble, B., Comeau, J., Patterson, J., & Needle, R. (1980). Family stress and coping: A decade review. *Journal of Marriage and the Family, 42*, 855-871.

McCubbin, H. I., & Patterson, J. (1982). Family adaptation to crises. In H. I. McCubbin (Ed.), *Family stress, coping and social support* (pp. 26-47). Springfield, IL: Charles C Thomas.

McCubbin, H., & Patterson, M. (1983). The family stress process. In H. McCubbin, M. Sussman, & J. Patterson (Eds.), *Social stress and the family.* New York: Haworth.

McLain, R., & Weigert, A. (1979). Toward a phenomenological sociology of the family: A programmatic essay. In W. R. Burr, R. Hill, F. I. Nye, & I. Reiss (Eds.), *Contemporary theories about the family* (Vol. 2). New York: Free Press.

Mead, H. (1953). *Types and problems of philosophy.* New York: Holt.

Montgomery, J., & Fewer, W. (1988). *Family systems and beyond.* New York: Human Sciences.

Morgaine, C. A. (1992). Alternative paradigms for helping families change themselves. *Family Relations, 41*, 12-17.

Neff, P. (1982). *Tough love.* Nashville, TN: Abingdon.

Neuman, W. L. (1991). *Social research methods.* Boston: Allyn & Bacon.

Nye, F. I., & Berardo, F. M. (1966). *Emerging conceptual frameworks in family analysis.* New York: Macmillan.

Olson, D. H. (1976). Bridging research, theory, and application: The triple threat in science. In D. Olson (Ed.), *Treating relationships.* Lake Mills, MN: Graphic.

Olson, D. H., Sprenkle, D. H., & Russell, C. S. (1979). Circumplex model of marital and family systems: I. Cohesion, adaptability dimensions, family types, and clinical applications. *Family Process, 18*, 3-28.

Osmond, M. W. (1981). *Rethinking family sociology from a radical-critical perspective: Applications and implications.* Paper presented at National Council on Family Relations, Milwaukee, WI.

Paolucci, B., Hall, O. A., & Axinn, N. (1977). *Family decision making: An ecosystem approach.* New York: John Wiley.

Pearlin, L. I., & Schooler, C. (1978). The structure of coping. *Journal of Health and Social Behavior, 19,* 2-21.

Pearlin, L. I., & Schooler, C. (1982). The structure of coping. In H. I. McCubbin (Ed.), *Family stress, coping and social support* (pp. 109-135). Springfield, IL: Charles C Thomas.

Plag, J. (1974, April). *Proposal for the long-term follow-up of returned prisoners of war, their families and the families of servicemen missing in action: A basis for the delivery of health care services.* Paper presented at the POW Research Consultants Conference, San Diego, CA.

Reiss, D. (1981). *The family's construction of reality.* Cambridge, MA: Harvard University Press.

Reiss, D., & Oliveri, M. E. (1991). The family's conception of accountability and competence: A new approach to the conceptualization of family stress. *Family Process, 30,* 193-214.

Rousseau, J. J. (1750). Discourse on the sciences and arts. In R. D. Masters (Ed.), *The first and second discourses* (1964). New York: St. Martin's.

Rousseau, J. J. (1762). *Emile, or education* (1948 Trans. by B. Foxley). London: J. M. Dent.

Schutz, A. (1967). *The phenomenology of the social world.* Evanston, IL: Northwestern University Press.

Schutz, A. (1970). *On phenomenology and social relations: Selected writings* (H. R. Wagner, Ed.). Chicago: University of Chicago Press.

Sluzki, C. E. (1983). Process, structure and world views: Toward an integrated view of systemic models in family therapy. *Family Process, 22,* 469-476.

Sprey, J. (Ed.). (1990). *Fashioning family theory.* Newbury Park, CA: Sage.

Steinglass, P., Bennett, L. A., Wolin, S. J., & Reiss, D. (1987). *The alcoholic family.* New York: Basic Books.

Thomas, D. L., & Wilcox, J. E. (1987). The rise of family theory: Critiques from philosophy of science and hermeneutics. In M. Sussman & S. Steinmetz (Eds.), *Handbook on marriage and the family.* New York: Plenum.

Walker, A. J. (1985). Reconceptualizing family stress. *Journal of Marriage and the Family, 47,* 827-837.

Walker, A. J., Martin, S.S.K., & Thompson, L. (1988). Feminist programs for families. *Family Relations, 37,* 17-22.

Waller, W. W. (1938). *The family: A dynamic interpretation.* New York: Cordan.

Watzlawick, P., Beavin, J., & Jackson, D. D. (1967). *Pragmatics of human communication: A study of interactional patterns, pathologies, and paradoxes.* New York: Norton.

Watzlawick, P., Weakland, J. H., & Fisch, R. (1974). *Change: Principles of problem formation and problem resolution.* New York: Norton.

Williams, R. W., & Olson, T. D. (1989). *An alternative starting point for family theory.* Unpublished paper presented at meeting of National Council on Family Relations, New Orleans, LA.

Author Index

Subject Index

ABC-X model, 3, 30-32, 37-39, 50, 129, 195
Allocation of resources, 81, 86-92, 197
  independent patterns, 87, 88-91
  parallel, 87, 89, 91
  reciprocal, 87-88, 91
Antithesis, 10, 12-23
  interpretive paradigm, 18
Aspects of family systems, 4, 41, 94-97
  communication, 4-5, 41, 61, 96, 100, 102, 112, 114-115, 198-199
  contention, 5, 41, 61, 96, 100-101, 122-124
  daily routines and chores, 4, 41, 61, 96, 100, 102, 106-108
  emotional climate, 4, 41, 61, 96, 100-102, 108-111
  family development, 5, 41, 61, 96, 100-101, 120-122
  family rituals and celebrations, 4, 41, 61, 95, 100, 102, 117-120
  leadership and decision making, 4, 41, 61, 96, 100, 103, 114-117
  marital satisfaction, 4-5, 41, 61, 94-97, 99-101, 104-106
  togetherness and cohesion, 4-5, 41, 61, 96, 100, 102, 110-113, 198-199

Bankruptcy, 54-55, 82-83, 104-127, 151, 155, 160, 162, 164, 166-167, 171-173, 177
Basic assumptions, 3
Boundary ambiguity, 31, 36

Chronically ill children, 54, 57, 82-83, 104-127, 151, 154, 158, 162, 164, 166-171, 173-174
Cognitive coping strategies:
  blaming, 139
  reframing, 140
Complexity of family responses, 194-196
Conceptual framework of coping strategies, 131-133
Coping processes, 45
Coping resources, 128-130, 132
Coping strategies, 2, 5-6, 31, 38, 41-42, 128-177, 200-202
  bankruptcy, 184-185, 187-188
  chronic stress, 189-190, 203
  cognition, 132-134, 137-140, 155-159, 172-173, 176
  communication, 132-133, 135-136, 143-145, 159-161, 172-173, 201-202

About the Authors

Robert G. Burr is a teacher/coordinator for the LDS Church Education System. He lives in San Bernardino, California, with his wife Cheryl and their four sons. He received a Family Science undergraduate degree as well as a Family Life Education master's degree from Brigham Young University. He received his Ph.D. in Marriage and Family Therapy from Texas Tech University.

Wesley R. Burr (Ph.D.) is a professor in the department of Family Sciences at Brigham Young University. He received his Ph.D. from the University of Minnesota in 1967. He has also taught at Portland State University, University of Wisconsin, University of Nebraska, the University of Exeter in England, and Arizona State University. The main emphasis in his scholarship has been in the development and application of theories about the family. He has written or edited 15 books and numerous articles in professional journals. His most recent book is *Family Science* (1993) with Randal Day and Kathleen Bahr. He has been involved with a number of professional organizations and served as president of the National Council on Family Relations (NCFR) in 1982. He also has directed many marriage and family enrichment programs, and lectures widely in the United Sates and Europe on family theories and methods of improving family life.

Cynthia Doxey studied Child and Family Development and Family Ecology at the University of Utah where she received her B.A. and M.A. degrees. Her research focused on families' influence on musically gifted children. She received a Master of Philosophy degree at Cambridge University in England where she studied education, again with an emphasis on children's musical and intellectual abilities. Currently, she is completing her Ph.D. in Family Studies at Brigham Young University where she has participated in research on family stress, and also has examined the family-of-origin factors that influence early marital unity and happiness. Although she has lived in Utah for much of her life, experiences of living in Spain and England for several years have broadened her interest in families from different cultures.

Brent Harker expects to complete his doctoral dissertation on loving behaviors and family functioning in 1994. In 1987, he completed a master's degree in Public Administration. His interests include family stress, family systems theory, loving behaviors, and family assessment using Olson's Circumplex Model. His career away from home has involved journalism and public relations, while his career at home focuses on working with his wife to raise five children.

Thomas B. Holman (Ph.D.) is an Associate Professor of Family Sciences and director of the Family Studies and Human Development Interdepartmental Doctoral Program at Brigham Young University. His scholarly interests are in the area of religion, mate selection, marital quality, and qualitative research. His recent publications include the treatise on marriage in the *Encyclopedia of Mormonism* and articles on religious behavior, marital satisfaction, sexual behavior, and attitudes toward family and career. His current research is a qualitative longitudinal study of Mormon dating, mate selection, and the transition into marriage.

Shirley R. Klein (Ph.D.) is an Assistant Professor of Family Sciences at Brigham Young University. She received a bachelor's degree in Home Economics Education at the University of Arizona, a master's degree in Home Economics Education at Brigham Young University, and a doctoral degree in Cultural Foundations of Education from the University of Utah. She has authored articles about the implication of women's changing roles for family life education and stress in family systems. She has directed curriculum projects for the Utah State Office of Education and the Department of Corrections.

Paul H. Martin received his B.S. degree in Family Science from Brigham Young University in 1990. He is completing his M.S. degree in Family Life Education also at BYU. Paul has had various opportunities working with people, young and old, who experience stress in their lives. Previous positions held include: a psychiatric aide in a state hospital; a teacher of elementary, high school, and university students; a supervisor of mentally and physically handicapped adults; a homeless employment specialist; and he is currently a family life educator and case manager of homeless and low-income families in Provo, Utah.

Russell L. McClure earned a bachelor's degree in Sociology at BYU and earned a Master of Education degree in Educational Psychology in 1986. He will soon complete a Ph.D. in Family Science. His interests include family stress, intergenerational processes, and family loving. His dissertation will focus on wives of clergymen.

Shawna Weiler Parrish received a B.A. in Family Living from Brigham Young University and is currently raising her son while her husband completes his medical school training. She plans to continue her education and would like to research and conduct interviews with women concerning pregnancy.

Daniel A. Stuart received his bachelor's degree in Family Science and his master's degree in Marriage and Family Therapy from Brigham Young University. His work on the Family Stress Management Project earned him the BYU Undergraduate Research and Creative Works Award in 1993. He is now a practicing Marriage and Family Therapist at the Family Preservation Institute in Logan, Utah.

Alan C. Taylor received a bachelor's degree at Brigham Young University with an emphasis in Family Life Education. He currently is working toward a doctorate degree in the Family Science area. He has presented several workshops about family stress and self-esteem to various high school groups and women's organizations. He has also been involved in other research projects involving household chores with dual earner couples.

Mark S. White received his B.S. from Brigham Young University in the field of Family Science. Mark currently is finishing his master's degree in Family Studies with an emphasis in Marriage and Family Therapy at the University of Kentucky. Upon graduation in December of 1993, he plans to practice in Minnesota as a Marriage and Family Therapist.